easy everyday

simple recipes for no-fuss food

RYLAND
PETERS
& SMALL

LONDON NEW YORK

Senior Designer Toni Kay

Editor Céline Hughes

Picture Research Emily Westlake

Production Toby Marshall

Art Director Leslie Harrington

Publishing Director Alison Starling

Indexer Penelope Kent

First published in the United States
in 2008 by Ryland Peters & Small, Inc.
519 Broadway, 5th Floor
New York, NY 10012
www.rylandpeters.com

10 9 8 7 6 5 4 3 2 1

Text © Ghillie Basan, Fiona Beckett,
Susannah Blake, Tamsin Burnett-Hall,
Maxine Clark, Linda Collister, Tonia
George, Brian Glover, Rachael Anne Hill,
Jennifer Joyce, Caroline Marson, Jane
Noraika, Louise Pickford, Jennie
Shapter, Sonia Stevenson, Linda Tubby,
Fran Warde, Laura Washburn, and
Ryland Peters & Small 2008

Design and photographs
© Ryland Peters & Small 2008

ISBN: 978-1-84597-634-7

The recipes in this book have been
published previously by Ryland Peters
& Small, Inc.

Printed and bound in China

Library of Congress Cataloging-in-
Publication Data

Easy everyday : simple recipes for
no-fuss food.
    p. cm.
  Includes index.
  ISBN 978-1-84597-634-7
  1. Quick and easy cookery.
  TX833.5.E2788 2008
  641.5'55--dc22

                                    2007044142

Notes:

• All spoon measurements are level, unless otherwise specified.

• Ovens should be preheated to the specified temperature.
Recipes in this book were tested using a regular oven. If using
a convection oven, follow the manufacturer's instructions for
adjusting temperatures.

• All eggs are medium, unless otherwise specified. Recipes
containing raw or partially cooked egg, or raw fish or shellfish,
should not be served to the very young, very old, anyone with
a compromised immune system, or pregnant women.

easy everyday

CONTENTS

When you've had a busy day or you've just come home from work, the last thing you want to do is spend your evening in the kitchen cooking up a storm. Although it's all too tempting to buy a ready-meal on the way home or order a takeout, nothing beats a freshly made, homecooked meal. Flick through *Easy Everyday* and you will find plenty of delicious, easy recipes to inspire you whether you are feeding a whole hungry family or just one other person. And with all sorts of dishes, from soups and quick snacks to hearty entrées and scrumptious desserts, there's an idea here for every occasion.

You don't have to scour the supermarket for obscure ingredients or slave over a hot stove for hours to make the recipes in this book. Every one is designed to be simple, satisfying, and hassle-free—perfect for every day. Some are super-quick for when the family's clamoring for their dinner; others require minimum preparation followed by an hour or so in the oven so that you can get on with your evening while dinner's cooking.

You won't just have the evening meal covered with *Easy Everyday*—there are salads and lunchboxes to help you make lunches that both you and the children will love. And the chapter on drinks lets you try some fresh, healthy herbal teas, juices, and smoothies.

Everyone can make easy everyday food with the help of these fantastic recipes. Tuck in and try one today!

INTRODUCTION

SOUPS

This marvelous dish is aromatherapy in a soup. Purée it coarsely, so the brilliant carrot orange is just flecked with green. The bocconcini—*little mouthfuls of mini-mozzarellas—peep out from just under the surface. Sprinkle with Chinese flowering chives if you can find them, otherwise regular chives are just fine.*

herb and carrot soup

3 thin leeks, thinly sliced

2 garlic cloves, crushed

1 tablespoon peanut or safflower oil

1¼ lb. young carrots, well scrubbed and thinly sliced

5 cups vegetable stock or water

1 cup fresh sorrel, stalks removed and leaves chopped

leaves from 4 fresh tarragon sprigs

leaves from 6 fresh parsley sprigs

leaves from 4 fresh basil sprigs

leaves from 6 fresh marjoram sprigs

TO SERVE

100 ml sour cream

12 bocconcini, torn in half, or 2 mozzarellas, torn into pieces

a handful of Chinese flowering chives (kuchai), or regular chives

freshly ground black pepper

SERVES 6

Put the leeks, garlic, and oil in a small saucepan, cover with a lid, and cook gently for 5 minutes. Add the carrots and cook gently for a further 5 minutes. Add the stock or water, bring to a boil, and simmer for 5 minutes. Lower the heat, add the sorrel, and simmer, uncovered, for a further 5 minutes.

Coarsely chop the tarragon, parsley, basil, and marjoram. Stir into the soup. Strain the mixture through a strainer into a clean pan and put the solids into a food processor or blender with a little of the liquid. Blend to a coarse purée, then return to the pan and reheat.

Remove from the heat and fold in the sour cream. Ladle into hot bowls and add a few *bocconcini* pieces to each one. Sprinkle with chive flowers or regular chives and pepper, then serve.

An old-fashioned, nourishing soup, full of healthy green things. If you cannot find sorrel in your local supermarket, it can be omitted.

kitchen garden soup

1 fresh bay leaf

1 small cabbage, quartered

4 tablespoons unsalted butter

2 leeks, halved and sliced

1 onion, chopped

2 teaspoons salt

8 oz. new potatoes, chopped

a handful of fresh flatleaf parsley, chopped

8 oz. fresh shelled peas

1 romaine lettuce heart, quartered and sliced thinly

a handful of fresh sorrel, sliced

sea salt and freshly ground black pepper

unsalted butter and/or sour cream, to serve (optional)

SERVES 4–6

Put the bay leaf in a large saucepan of water and bring to a boil. Add the cabbage quarters and blanch for 3 minutes. Drain the cabbage, pat dry, and slice thinly.

Heat the butter in a large saucepan. Add the cabbage, leeks, onion, and 2 teaspoons salt and cook until softened, 5–10 minutes. Add the potatoes, parsley, and 2 quarts water. Season to taste and simmer gently for 40 minutes.

Stir in the peas, lettuce, and sorrel and cook for 10 minutes more. Taste for seasoning. Ladle into bowls, add 1 tablespoon butter and/or sour cream, if using, to each, and serve.

golden butternut squash soup

1½ lb. butternut squash, peeled

2 tablespoons olive oil

2 onions, diced

1 garlic clove, crushed

6 cups chicken or vegetable stock

sea salt and freshly ground
black pepper

light cream, to serve (optional)

SERVES 4

Squash is a wonderfully versatile vegetable, and it's used to great effect in this flavorful soup.

Cut the squash in half lengthwise and use a spoon to scoop out the seeds. Chop the flesh into 1-inch pieces.

Heat the oil in a large saucepan, add the squash, onions, and garlic, and sauté over low heat for 10 minutes. Add the stock, bring to a boil, then simmer for 30 minutes.

Using a handheld blender, blitz the soup until smooth and creamy. Season and serve with a drizzle of cream, if liked.

flag bean soup

1 tablespoon olive oil, plus extra to taste

3 large garlic cloves: 2 cut into slices and 1 crushed

1 large onion, finely chopped

1 heaping cup French green lentils, preferably Le Puy, rinsed

4 cups boiling chicken or vegetable stock, plus extra to taste

½ cup canned butter beans

1 cup canned green flageolet beans

1 cup canned red kidney beans

1 cup canned haricot or cannellini beans

sea salt and freshly ground black pepper

TO SERVE

fresh parsley or basil leaves

basil oil or olive oil, to drizzle

grated lemon peel (optional)

crusty bread

SERVES 4

This flag bean soup is so-called because the beans are red, green, and white, the color of the Italian flag. It's exactly the sort of soup you need on a cold winter's day. Using canned beans, it takes no time at all to prepare, and you can use vegetable or chicken stock to suit either vegetarians or meat-eaters.

Heat the olive oil in a skillet, add the sliced garlic, and fry gently on both sides until crisp and golden. Remove and drain on paper towels.

Put the onion and crushed garlic in the skillet, adding extra oil if necessary, and cook gently until softened and transparent. Add the lentils and half the stock and cook until the lentils are just tender.

Meanwhile, rinse and drain all the beans. Put them in a strainer and dunk the strainer in a large saucepan of boiling water. The beans are cooked—you are just reheating them.

Add the hot beans to the lentils and add the remaining stock. Taste, and add salt and pepper as necessary. If the soup is too thick, add extra boiling stock or water. Ladle into bowls, top with the reserved fried garlic and the herbs, drizzle with a few drops of basil oil, and top with lemon peel, if using. Serve with crusty bread.

The tastiest meals are often the very simplest. To make truly wholesome tomato soup, all you need is fresh tomato sauce, thinned down with stock, heated until almost but not quite boiling (otherwise it loses its fresh taste), then finished off with lemon juice and peel and a spoonful of pesto.

tomato soup

2 lb. very ripe red tomatoes

2 cups chicken stock, or to taste

sea salt and coarsely crushed black pepper

grated peel and freshly squeezed juice of 1 unwaxed lemon

¼ cup pesto, to serve

SERVES 4

To peel the tomatoes, cut a cross in the base of each and dunk into a saucepan of boiling water. Remove after 10 seconds and transfer to a strainer set over a large saucepan. Slip off and discard the skins and cut the tomatoes in half around their "equators." Using a teaspoon, seed into the strainer, then press the pulp and juice through the strainer and add to a blender. Discard the seeds. Chop the tomato halves and add to the blender. Alternatively, put through a mouli food mill.

Purée the tomatoes, adding a little of the stock to help the process—you may have to work in batches. Add the remaining stock, season to taste, and transfer to the saucepan. Heat well without boiling. Serve in heated soup plates topped with a spoonful of lemon juice, pesto, lemon peel, and pepper.

cream of broccoli soup
with leeks and fava beans

2 large leeks, halved and sliced

2 tablespoons butter

2 tablespoons safflower oil

2 large heads broccoli, broken into florets

1 medium baking potato, chopped

2¾ cups vegetable or chicken stock

1 cup shelled fava beans, fresh or frozen

sea salt and freshly ground white pepper

basil or parsley oil, to serve

SERVES 4

A pale green, fresh, summery soup that can be adapted to other ingredients—it's also good with cauliflower and cannellini beans, or sweet potatoes and fresh borlottis. Feel free to use frozen fava beans. Like peas and corn, they are one of the few ingredients that can be better frozen. Picked and frozen almost immediately, their sugars have no time to turn to starch.

Put the butter and oil in a large saucepan and heat until the butter melts. Add the leeks and fry gently until softened but not brown. Reserve a few spoonfuls of the cooked leeks for garnish.

Add the broccoli to the pan and stir-fry until bright green. Add the potato and stock and bring to a boil. Reduce the heat, season, and simmer for 30 minutes, topping up with boiling water if necessary.

If using frozen fava beans, cook in boiling salted water until just tender, then drain and transfer to a bowl of cold water. Pop the cooked beans out of their grey skins and discard the skins—the bright green beans look and taste better. Reserve a few spoonfuls of fava beans for serving.

Strain the soup into a bowl and put the solids and remaining fava beans in a blender or food processor. Add 2 ladles of the strained liquid and purée until smooth. Add the remaining liquid and blend again. If the soup is too thick, thin it with water. Reheat the soup, pour into heated soup bowls, top with the reserved leeks and skinned fava beans, then serve with a trickle of basil or parsley oil over the top.

soupe au pistou

¼ cup olive oil

1 red onion, cut into wedges

1 large potato,
cut into ½-inch cubes

a handful of soup pasta,
such as orecchiette
(or the traditional vermicelli)

4 cups chicken or vegetable stock

1 cup cooked or canned cannellini
beans, rinsed and drained

4 baby carrots, halved or
quartered lengthwise

2 cups Brussels sprouts, halved,
or baby zucchini,
cut into thick slices

1 red bell pepper, peeled, cored,
and sliced

1¾ cups fresh shelled peas

sea salt and freshly ground
black pepper

PISTOU

leaves from a handful of fresh basil

2 garlic cloves, crushed

olive oil (see method)

SERVES 4

Pistou is the Provençal version of pesto, and to make it you need a big bunch of scented summertime basil. Unlike pesto, it doesn't contain pine nuts or cheese. This version of the soup is quicker to cook than the traditional one. If you'd like the classic, cook it all together—beans first; then root vegetables and pasta; then fresh peas, followed by leafy things. Red kidney beans are often included, but this version uses white beans instead.

To make the *pistou*, put the basil and garlic in a blender or food processor and blend as finely as possible. Add enough olive oil in a steady stream to form a loose paste. Set aside.

Heat the oil in a small skillet, add the onion wedges, and fry gently on both sides until softened. Cook the potato and soup pasta in salted boiling water until tender. Drain. Blanch your choice of carrots, sprouts, zucchini, bell pepper, and peas, in salted boiling water until tender but crisp, about 3–5 minutes. Drain and refresh in cold water.

Bring the stock to a boil and add the seasoning, pasta, and all the vegetables including the cannellini beans. Simmer for 2 minutes or until heated through.

Serve in heated soup plates, with a separate bowl of *pistou*. Let people stir the *pistou* into their own soup to taste.

alphabet soup

4 oz. smoked pancetta or prosciutto, cubed

1 tablespoon olive oil

½ onion, chopped

1 large potato, cubed and rinsed

1 carrot, quartered lengthwise, then sliced crosswise into triangles

2 celery stalks, sliced

2 small zucchini, quartered lengthwise, then sliced crosswise into triangles

3 tomatoes, halved, seeded, and chopped

4 cups chicken stock

2–3 cups alfabetto soup pasta

½ small round cabbage, quartered, cored, and sliced

1 cup green beans, cut into 1-inch lengths

1 cup peas, fresh or frozen

1 cup canned beans, such as cannellini, red kidney, or chickpeas, rinsed and drained

sea salt and freshly ground black pepper

TO SERVE

2 tablespoons freshly chopped parsley

crusty Italian bread

freshly grated cheddar cheese

SERVES 4

Beloved of children everywhere, alphabet pasta can be added to all sorts of other soups, but is especially useful with vegetable soups, to encourage little ones to eat their greens. The bacon and chicken stock make the soup flavorful, but if you would like to stay vegetarian, use a well-flavored vegetable stock and a few spoonfuls of crushed tomatoes.

Put the pancetta or prosciutto in a large saucepan, heat gently, and fry until the fat runs. Add the olive oil, heat briefly, then add the onion and cook gently until softened but not brown.

Add the potato, carrot, celery, zucchini, tomatoes, and some seasoning. Add the stock and pasta and heat until simmering. Cook over low heat for about 15 minutes. Add the cabbage and beans, bring to a boil, and cook for 5 minutes, then add the peas and canned beans and cook for another 2–3 minutes until all the vegetables are tender. Season to taste, sprinkle with parsley, then serve with bread and cheese (shown here melted on top of the bread).

japanese fresh corn soup
with scallions and soy sauce

4 ears of fresh corn or
2 cups fresh corn kernels

4 cups hot chicken stock

4 egg yolks

4 scallions, sliced diagonally

2 tablespoons dark soy sauce

cracked pepper, or a Japanese
pepper mixture, such as furikake
seasoning or seven-spice

SERVES 4

This is a variation on a traditional Japanese summer soup, prized for the fresh taste of corn—and very easy to make.

Bring a large saucepan of water to a boil, add the corn, and simmer for about 2 minutes. Drain. Hold the corn upright on a cutting board, blunt end down. Run a sharp knife down the cobs, shaving off the kernels. Reserve a few sliced-off sections of kernels for serving, blanching them in boiling water for 2 minutes.

Put the remaining kernels in a blender with 1 cup of the stock. Purée until smooth, then press through a fine-mesh sieve into a saucepan. Return the corn to the blender, add another ladle of stock, purée, then strain as before, pushing through as much corn juice as possible. Repeat until all the stock has been used. Reheat the mixture, then remove from the heat.

Put 1 egg yolk into each of 4 small soup bowls, ladle the soup on top and beat with chopsticks (the hot soup cooks the egg). Alternatively, you can beat all 4 egg yolks in a mixing bowl first, then beat into the soup and ladle into bowls. Serve topped with scallions, the reserved kernel sections, soy sauce, and pepper to taste.

laksa

3 tablespoons peanut oil

2 cups canned coconut milk

2 boneless chicken breasts, skinned and thickly sliced

fish sauce or salt, to taste

1½ lb. fresh or 4 oz. dried udon noodles

SPICE PASTE

3–6 red or orange chiles, cored and chopped

1 shallot, chopped

2 lemon grass stalks, finely sliced

1 inch fresh ginger, finely sliced

½ teaspoon ground turmeric

6 blanched almonds, chopped

1 tablespoon fish sauce or a pinch of salt

1 garlic clove, crushed

TO SERVE

1 small package fresh bean sprouts, trimmed, rinsed, and drained

4 scallions, sliced diagonally

1 red chile, cored and finely sliced

cilantro (optional)

SERVES 4

Laksas are spicy soups from Malaysia, Indonesia, and the Philippines, though the Malay ones are the best known. They generally contain vegetables, shrimp, pork, and noodles, but this varies from region to region. This one contains chicken, but feel free to use fish or other seafood instead. The spice paste is the key—usually laboriously made with a mortar and pestle, a blender is an easy alternative.

Put all the spice paste ingredients into a spice grinder or blender and work to a paste (add a little water if necessary).

Heat the oil in a wok, add the spice paste, and cook gently for about 5 minutes until aromatic. Add the thick part of the coconut milk (if any) and stir-fry until it releases its oil, then add the thinner part and heat gently. Add 4 cups water and bring to a boil. Add the chicken, reduce the heat, and poach gently without boiling until the meat is cooked through, about 10–15 minutes. Add the fish sauce or salt, to taste.

If using fresh noodles, rinse in cold water, then boil for about 1–2 minutes. If using dried noodles, cook in unsalted boiling water for 3–5 minutes, or until done, then drain. Divide the noodles between large soup bowls. Add the chicken and liquid, top with the bean sprouts, scallions, chile, and cilantro, if using, and serve.

This super-healthy chunky soup is full of interesting flavors. Lentils give the soup color and texture, but they also pack a powerful protein punch while helping to reduce cholesterol.

smoked haddock and green lentil chowder

¾ cup French green lentils, preferably Le Puy, rinsed

2 leeks, rinsed and chopped

2½ cups vegetable, fish, or chicken stock

8 small new potatoes, scrubbed and diced

1¼ cups skim milk

12 oz. smoked haddock fillets, skinned

sea salt and freshly ground black pepper

2 tablespoons scissor-snipped fresh chives, to serve

SERVES 4

Put the rinsed lentils in a saucepan, add enough boiling water to cover the lentils by 1½ inches, cover the saucepan, and simmer for 15–20 minutes until tender, then drain.

Meanwhile, simmer the leeks in ¼ cup of the stock in a large saucepan, covered, for 3–4 minutes until softened. Stir in the potatoes, milk, and remaining stock. Season and bring to a boil, then simmer for 15 minutes or until the potatoes are tender.

Add the smoked haddock to the saucepan and simmer for 4–5 minutes until the fish flakes easily. Lift the haddock out of the pan and break into large flakes.

Stir the lentils into the chowder, ladle into bowls, and top with the flaked smoked haddock. Add a scattering of chives and serve.

chicken soup

1 tablespoon olive oil

1 onion, chopped

1 garlic clove, crushed

2 chicken breasts, diced

2 leeks, chopped

2 medium potatoes, unpeeled and chopped

5 cups chicken stock

3 fresh thyme sprigs

2 bay leaves

kernels from 1 ear of corn

sea salt and freshly ground black pepper

SERVES 4

A bowlful of this comforting soup makes everyone feel better, especially when served with a slab of warm crusty bread.

Heat the olive oil in a saucepan, add the onion, garlic, chicken, and leeks, and sauté gently for 8 minutes without browning. Add the potatoes, stock, thyme, and bay leaves, then season and simmer for 20 minutes.

Add the corn kernels and cook for a further 10 minutes. Remove the thyme and bay leaves before serving.

sausage soup

1½ lb. fresh pork sausages, such as bratwurst, pricked with a fork

3 onions, chopped

3 tomatoes, peeled (see page 19), seeded, and chopped

olive oil, to sprinkle

8 oz. smoked pancetta or prosciutto, coarsely chopped

2 garlic cloves, crushed with a pinch of salt

a large fresh sage sprig, sliced

1 baguette, sliced

8 oz. cheese, such as cheddar, coarsely grated

sea salt and freshly ground black pepper

freshly chopped parsley, to serve (optional)

SERVES 4

Here's a deliciously satisfying soup from the south of France. It serves four as a simple winter meal, but it can easily be made more substantial by adding the suggestions in the note below.

Preheat the oven to 400°F.

Arrange the sausages in a ring around a large, shallow, flameproof casserole dish or baking dish. Put the onions and tomatoes in the middle and sprinkle with olive oil. Cook in the preheated oven until done (about 30 minutes, depending on the thickness of the sausages). Stir the onions and tomatoes after 15–20 minutes to stop them burning. Leave the oven on.

When the sausages are done, remove, cut into 3–4 pieces each, and set aside. Put the dish on top of the stove and add the pancetta. Fry, stirring, until crisp, and the fat is starting to run. Add the garlic and fry for about 1 minute, then add the sage. Add about 4 cups water and stir. Taste and adjust the seasoning, adding extra water if the mixture is too thick.

Meanwhile, put the slices of baguette on a baking sheet and cook at the top of the oven until golden. Remove from the oven and sprinkle with grated cheese. Return to the oven until the cheese has melted and become almost crisp. To serve, put about 3 cheese-topped croutes in 4 soup plates, ladle in the soup, and top with the sausages. Sprinkle with parsley, if using, and serve.

Notes

• If you like, serve the croutes separately. Adding them at the end keeps them crisp to the last possible moment, though the method of pouring the soup over them is traditionally French.

• The pancetta may be omitted, but the soup will need more seasoning. Other vegetables such as quartered and sliced zucchini or cabbage may also be used.

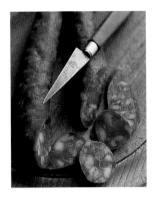

It seems that most dishes containing chorizo taste pretty good. This soup is no exception and needs no embellishments, making it refreshingly simple to prepare. Make sure you buy the correct chorizo—you want the short, fat, little cured sausages. They are ready to eat but are so much better when they are fried and crispy.

chickpea, tomato, and chorizo soup

6 oz. chorizo, roughly chopped

1 red onion, chopped

2 garlic cloves, crushed

a 14-oz. can chopped plum tomatoes

2 fresh thyme sprigs

a 14-oz. can chickpeas, drained and rinsed

4 cups vegetable stock

sea salt and freshly ground black pepper

SERVES 4

Put the chorizo in a large saucepan or casserole dish over medium heat and cook until it starts to release its oil. Continue to cook, stirring, for 4–5 minutes until it is lovely and crisp.

Add the red onion and garlic and turn the heat right down to allow them to soften in the chorizo's paprika-infused oil. After 6–7 minutes the onion and garlic should be translucent and glossy. Add the tomatoes and thyme and turn the heat back up. Cook for 5 minutes to intensify the flavor, then add the chickpeas and stock. Return to a boil, cover, and simmer for 15 minutes.

Remove the thyme. Season well and simmer for a further 10 minutes to allow all the flavors to get to know one another.

Transfer to bowls and serve.

LUNCHBOXES & SALADS

The spices and flavorings used in this recipe are typical of North African cooking, and all over the region, pita bread is stuffed with grilled meat, salad, and yogurt. Use other ground meats if you prefer.

2 teaspoons coriander seeds

1 teaspoon cumin seeds

2 tablespoons extra virgin olive oil

1 onion, finely chopped

2 garlic cloves, crushed

1 teaspoon ground cinnamon

¼–½ teaspoon cayenne pepper

10 oz. ground lamb

a pinch of salt

2 tablespoons freshly chopped cilantro leaves

4 pita breads

a few salad leaves, such as romaine lettuce and watercress

plain yogurt or tahini sauce

1 tablespoon sesame seeds, toasted in a dry skillet

SERVES 4

lamb in pita bread

Put the coriander seeds and cumin seeds into a small dry skillet and fry until they start to brown and release their aroma. Let cool slightly, then grind to powder in a spice grinder (use a clean coffee grinder) or with a mortar and pestle.

Heat the oil in a skillet, add the onion, garlic, ground coriander, cumin, and cinnamon, and the pepper and fry gently for 5 minutes until softened but not golden. Increase the heat, add the lamb and the pinch of salt, and stir-fry for 5–8 minutes until well browned. Stir in the cilantro.

Meanwhile, lightly toast the pita bread and cut a long slit in the side of each one. Carefully fill with a few salad leaves, add the ground lamb mixture, a spoonful of yogurt or tahini, and sprinkle with sesame seeds. Serve hot.

The hummus in these wraps is a great source of monounsaturated fat—the sort that not only lowers your bad cholesterol, but also maintains and may even increase your good cholesterol. The wraps are dead easy to make so they're great for putting together first thing in the morning before you leave the house.

chicken and hummus wraps

2 tablespoons hummus

4 small wheat tortillas

1 large grilled chicken breast, cut into thin strips

½ small cucumber, cut into thin strips

4 medium romaine lettuce leaves, shredded

4 teaspoons chili oil or sweet chili sauce

sea salt and freshly ground black pepper

4 toothpicks

SERVES 2

Spread ½ tablespoon hummus over each tortilla. Put the strips of chicken and cucumber on top of the hummus, then top with the shredded lettuce.

Drizzle each wrap with 1 teaspoon chili oil or sweet chili sauce and season generously. Carefully roll up the tortillas and secure each one in place with a toothpick. Chill the wraps in the refrigerator until you are ready to eat.

Variation If you prefer a vegetarian alternative, use tomato slices and arugula leaves instead of the chicken.

simple vegetable quiche

1 storebought whole-wheat
pie crust

FILLING

3½ oz. broccoli,
divided into small florets

1 tablespoon olive oil

1 onion, finely chopped

1 small red bell pepper,
sliced into rings and seeded

1 medium carrot, grated

3 eggs

⅔ cup milk

¼ teaspoon freshly grated nutmeg

freshly ground black pepper,
to serve (optional)

SERVES 6–8

Kids love quiche and this meat-free version is a great way to increase your child's vegetable intake. Almost any vegetables can be used, so be creative. Ready-made pie crusts are available from health food stores. The finished quiche can be frozen for up to 1 month.

Preheat the oven to 400°F. Unwrap the pie crust and put it on a baking sheet.

Steam the broccoli florets over a saucepan of gently simmering water for 3 minutes. Plunge them into cold water and drain well.

Heat the oil in a nonstick skillet, add the onion, and fry gently for 5 minutes, stirring frequently. Transfer the onion to the pie crust, spreading it evenly over the base. Arrange the broccoli, bell pepper, and carrot on top of the onion. Put the eggs, milk, nutmeg, and black pepper in a bowl and beat well. Pour the mixture over the vegetables in the pie crust.

Bake in the preheated oven for 15 minutes. Reduce the temperature to 350°F and continue to bake for about 20 minutes until the filling is set.

Variations

• Sprinkle the quiche with a little grated cheese just before baking.

• Add 1 tablespoon canned cannellini beans to the filling.

• Replace the broccoli and carrot with about 6 oz. finely chopped, well drained, blanched spinach and 2½ oz. crumbled goat cheese.

double-decker bacon and turkey club sandwich

12 thick slices of white bread

4 tablespoons mayonnaise

8 slices of deli turkey

4 crisp leaves of Boston or butter lettuce

1 avocado, pitted, peeled, and thinly sliced

8 paper-thin red onion slices

8 bacon slices, cooked crisp

4 slices of beefsteak tomato

16 toothpicks

SERVES 4

The club is the ultimate sandwich; a toasted bread tower generously layered with meat, vegetables, and sometimes cheese. A truly special lunchtime treat.

Toast the bread, then spread one side of each piece of toast with the mayonnaise. Stack the turkey, lettuce, and avocado on 4 of these and top with another piece of toast.

Stack the red onion, bacon, and tomato over and top with the remaining toast. Cut the sandwich in half diagonally and then again diagonally in the opposite direction. Secure each quarter with a toothpick. Repeat with the other 3 sandwiches.

Baby spinach is essential for this recipe because the leaves wilt and soften quickly, so you needn't remove the stalks or chop the leaves. The pancetta adds a special depth of flavor. Like all frittatas, this one is wonderful for both picnics and packed lunches.

spinach and pancetta frittata

6 extra-large eggs

1 tablespoon extra virgin olive or safflower oil

125 g smoked pancetta, cubed, or bacon, cut into strips

4 scallions, chopped

1 garlic clove, finely chopped

1½ cups baby spinach

sea salt and freshly ground black pepper

a 12-inch heavy skillet (measure the base, not the top)

SERVES 4

Preheat the broiler to medium.

Break the eggs into a bowl and beat briefly with a fork. Season well.

Heat 1 tablespoon of the oil in the skillet. Add the pancetta or bacon and cook over medium heat for 3–4 minutes until it starts to brown.

Add the scallions, garlic, and spinach and stir-fry for 3–4 minutes or until the spinach has wilted and the scallions have softened.

Pour the egg mixture into the pan, quickly mix into the other ingredients, and stop stirring. Reduce to a low heat and cook for 8–10 minutes, or until the top is almost set. Slide under the preheated broiler to finish cooking the top. Cut into wedges and serve hot or cold.

A robust omelet packed full of goodness, this is a perfect recipe for using up small quantities of leftover vegetables, including ingredients such as broccoli, corn, fava beans, or mushrooms. This tortilla is best finished under the broiler to retain the lovely colors on the top when serving, but you can also turn it over in the skillet to finish cooking in the classic way.

hearty country-style tortilla

¼ cup extra virgin olive or safflower oil

3 medium potatoes, about 12 oz., peeled and cubed

1 onion, halved and sliced

about ½ cup green beans, trimmed and cut into three

4 asparagus spears, cut into 2-inch lengths

1 red bell pepper, quartered, seeded, and thinly sliced

3 oz. spicy chorizo, sliced

1 garlic clove, finely chopped

6 extra-large eggs

½ cup frozen peas

sea salt and freshly ground black pepper

a 12-inch heavy nonstick skillet (measure the base, not the top)

SERVES 4–6

Preheat the broiler to medium.

Heat 2 tablespoons of the oil in the skillet. Add the potatoes and cook over medium heat for 5 minutes. Add the onion and cook for 10 minutes or until the potatoes are almost tender, lifting and turning occasionally.

Meanwhile put the beans and asparagus in a saucepan of salted boiling water and cook for 5 minutes. Drain and refresh in cold water. Drain well.

Add the bell pepper, chorizo, asparagus, beans, and garlic to the potatoes and cook for 5 minutes, stirring frequently.

Break the eggs into a large bowl, season, and beat briefly with a fork. Mix in the peas and cooked vegetable mixture.

If necessary, wipe out the skillet with a paper towel, then add the remaining oil and heat until hot. Add the tortilla mixture, letting it spread evenly in the skillet.

Cook over medium-low heat for about 10 minutes until the bottom is golden brown and the top almost set. Slide under the preheated broiler to set and lightly brown the top. Transfer to a serving plate, cut into wedges, and serve hot or warm.

tortilla with artichokes and serrano ham

3 tablespoons extra virgin olive
or safflower oil

3 medium potatoes, about 12 oz.,
peeled and cubed

1 Spanish onion, chopped

5 extra-large eggs

2 cups canned artichoke hearts or
bottoms in water, well drained
and halved

2 tablespoons fresh thyme leaves

3–4 oz. thinly sliced serrano ham
or prosciutto, torn into strips

6–8 slices goat cheese log with
rind, about 4 oz. (optional)

sea salt and freshly ground
black pepper

*a 12-inch heavy nonstick skillet
(measure the base, not the top)*

SERVES 3–4

*Most tortillas are inverted onto a plate and returned
to the skillet to finish cooking. However, this tortilla
is topped with cured mountain ham and should be
finished under the broiler. For a truly extravagant
touch, add a few slices of goat cheese log, which
melts beautifully into the top of the tortilla.*

Preheat the broiler to medium.

Heat 2 tablespoons of the oil in the skillet. Add the potatoes and
cook over medium heat for 5 minutes. Add the onion and cook for
a further 10 minutes, lifting and turning occasionally, until just
tender. The potatoes and onions should not brown very much.

Meanwhile, break the eggs into a large bowl, season, and beat
briefly with a fork.

Add the artichokes, thyme, and about three-fourths of the ham
to the bowl of eggs. Add the potatoes and onion and stir gently.

Heat the remaining oil in the skillet. Add the tortilla mixture,
spreading it evenly in the skillet. Cook over medium-low heat for
about 6 minutes, then top with the remaining ham. Cook for a
further 4–5 minutes or until the bottom is golden brown and the
top almost set.

Add the goat cheese, if using, and slide under the preheated broiler
just to brown the top, about 2–3 minutes. Cut into wedges and
serve hot or warm.

saffron potato salad with sun-dried tomatoes and caper and basil dressing

1 lb. large, waxy, yellow-fleshed potatoes, peeled

a pinch of saffron threads, about 20

8 sun-dried tomatoes (the dry kind, not in oil)

CAPER AND BASIL DRESSING

⅓ cup extra virgin olive oil

3 tablespoons freshly chopped basil leaves, plus extra to serve

2 tablespoons salted capers, rinsed and chopped, if large

1–2 tablespoons freshly squeezed lemon juice, to taste

sea salt and freshly ground black pepper

SERVES 4

The potatoes absorb the glorious golden color and subtle flavor of the saffron as they simmer gently with the tomatoes. The sunny colors of this salad are beautiful—yellow from the saffron, red from the tomato, and green from the basil. If you can, serve this warm, as the heat will release the heady aromas of the basil and saffron.

Cut the potatoes into large chunks. Put in a saucepan, add enough cold water to just cover them, then add the saffron and sun-dried tomatoes. Bring slowly to a boil, then turn down the heat, cover, and simmer very gently for about 12 minutes until just tender. If the water boils too fast, the potatoes will start to disintegrate. Drain well.

Pick out the now plumped up sun-dried tomatoes and slice them thinly. Tip the potatoes into a large bowl and add the sliced tomatoes.

To make the dressing, put the oil, chopped basil, and capers in a small bowl. Add lemon juice and seasoning and mix well. Pour over the hot potatoes, mix gently, then serve hot or warm, scattered with extra basil leaves.

French green lentils are a must here as they do not collapse when cooked. They give the salad plenty of texture. You couldn't find an easier recipe.

lentil and baked tomato salad

2 cups French green lentils, preferably Le Puy, rinsed

8 oz. cherry tomatoes

½ cup pitted olives

2½ oz. Parmesan

2 tablespoons balsamic vinegar

sea salt and freshly ground black pepper

olive oil, for baking and dressing

SERVES 4

Preheat the oven to 250°F.

Put the lentils in a saucepan, cover with water, and bring to a boil. Lower the heat and simmer for 40 minutes, until soft.

Put the tomatoes on a nonstick baking sheet, drizzle 3 tablespoons olive oil over them, then bake in the preheated oven for 40 minutes.

Drain the lentils when cooked and put in a serving bowl. Add the tomatoes, olives, and seasoning. Shave the Parmesan over the top and drizzle with olive oil and balsamic vinegar. Lightly mix and serve.

Greek salads are so much part of the easy, Mediterranean style of eating—a bit of crisp, a bit of fiery, a few baby herbs, some vinegary olives (and Greece produces some of the best), and salty anchovies. Use Kalamata olives, but unpitted, because they have more flavor. Warn anyone who will be eating the salad that the olives have pits.

1 head iceberg lettuce, quartered and torn apart

about 8 oz. feta cheese, crumbled into big pieces, or cubed

1 cup Kalamata olives

2 red onions, halved, then sliced into petals

2 Kirby cucumbers, halved lengthwise, then thinly sliced diagonally

4 big ripe red tomatoes, cut into chunks

8 anchovies, or to taste

a few fresh oregano sprigs, torn

a few fresh mint sprigs, torn

GREEK DRESSING

⅓ cup extra virgin olive oil, preferably Greek

2 tablespoons freshly squeezed lemon juice

sea salt and freshly ground black pepper

SERVES 4

big greek salad

Put the lettuce in a big bowl. Add the cheese, olives, onions, cucumbers, and tomatoes.

To make the dressing, beat the olive oil, lemon juice, and some seasoning in a bowl, then pour onto the salad.

Top with the anchovies, oregano, and mint, and serve.

2 cups cooked or canned chickpeas, rinsed and drained

4 marinated artichoke hearts, well drained and halved

4 large sun-blushed tomatoes, (optional)

8 oz. very ripe cherry tomatoes, halved

8 scallions, sliced diagonally

a handful of fresh basil, torn

a small handful of fresh chives, scissor-snipped

leaves from a small handful of fresh flatleaf parsley, chopped

2 oz. Parmesan

1 tablespoon black pepper, cracked with a mortar and pestle

DIJON DRESSING

⅓ cup extra virgin olive oil

1 tablespoon freshly squeezed lemon juice or sherry vinegar

1 teaspoon Dijon mustard

1 small garlic clove, crushed

sea salt and freshly ground black pepper

SERVES 4

Chickpeas are the basis of some of the best salads and vegetable entrée accompaniments. Like all dried legumes, they drink up flavors, but unlike some, chickpeas can be relied upon not to fall apart. You can part-prepare them, so the dressing soaks into the chickpeas, then add the fresh ingredients just before serving. Sun-blushed tomatoes are available from Italian deli counters.

quick chickpea salad

To make the dressing, put the olive oil, lemon juice or vinegar, mustard, and garlic in a bowl and beat with a fork. Season to taste. Add the chickpeas, artichoke hearts, and sun-blushed tomatoes, if using, and toss in the dressing. Cover and chill for up to 4 hours.

When ready to serve, add the cherry tomatoes, scallions, basil, chives, and parsley. Stir gently, then shave the Parmesan over the top and sprinkle with the pepper.

Variations
• You can add any number of other ingredients, including olives, prosciutto, salami, or chorizo, canned or grilled fresh tuna, other vegetables, lettuces, or herbs, or your favorite spices.

• Instead of Dijon dressing, dress with basil oil or other herb oil. A few drops of chili oil in the dressing instead of the mustard give a different kind of fire.

tuscan panzanella

6 very ripe, flavorful tomatoes

2 garlic cloves, sliced into slivers

4 thick slices of day-old bread, preferably Italian-style, such as pugliese or ciabatta

about 4 inches cucumber, halved, seeded, and finely sliced diagonally

1 red onion, chopped

1 tablespoon freshly chopped flatleaf parsley

1/2–3/4 cup extra virgin olive oil

2 tablespoons white wine vinegar, cider vinegar, or sherry vinegar

a handful of fresh basil, torn

12 caperberries or 1/4 cup capers packed in brine, rinsed and drained

1 teaspoon balsamic vinegar (optional)

sea salt and freshly ground black pepper

SERVES 4

There are as many variations of this Tuscan bread salad as there are cooks—some old recipes don't even include tomatoes. The trick is to let the flavors blend well without allowing the bread to disintegrate into a mush. Always use the ripest, reddest, most flavorful tomatoes you can find—Brandywine is a favorite variety, or you could use one of the full-flavored heirloom varieties, such as Black Russian or Green Zebra, or at least an Italian plum tomato.

Preheat the oven to 350°F.

Cut the tomatoes in half, spike with the slivers of garlic, and roast in the preheated oven for about 1 hour, or until wilted and some of the moisture has evaporated.

Meanwhile, put the bread on an oiled stove-top grill pan and cook until lightly toasted and barred with grill marks on both sides. Tear or cut the toast into pieces and put into a salad bowl. Sprinkle with a little water until damp.

Add the tomatoes, cucumber, onion, parsley, and some seasoning. Sprinkle with the olive oil and vinegar, toss well, then set aside for about 1 hour to develop the flavors.

Add the basil leaves, caperberries or capers, and balsamic vinegar, if using, and serve.

1 egg, preferably free-range and organic

6 smallest leaves of romaine lettuce

½ tablespoon freshly squeezed lemon juice, plus 1 lemon cut into wedges, to serve (optional)

2 tablespoons extra virgin olive oil

3–4 canned anchovies, rinsed and drained

Parmesan shavings, at room temperature

sea salt and freshly ground black pepper

CROUTONS

1 thick slice of crusty white bread

2 tablespoons oil

1 garlic clove, crushed

SERVES 1

This is probably the most famous salad in the world and the perfect combination of salty, crispy crunch. It was invented by Italian chef Caesar Cardini in Tijuana, Mexico, in 1924. Note that this recipe serves one person but it's easily adapted to serve more.

caesar salad

To cook the egg, put it in a small saucepan and bring to a boil. Reduce the heat and simmer for 4–5 minutes. Remove from the heat and cover with cold water to stop it cooking further. Let cool a little, then peel. Cut into quarters just before serving.

To make the croutons, tear the bread into bite-size chunks, brush with the oil, and rub with the garlic. Cook on a preheated stovetop grill pan until crisply golden and barred with brown.

Put the lettuce into a large bowl add some seasoning and the lemon juice and toss with your hands. Finally, sprinkle with olive oil and toss again.

Put the croutons in a bowl and put the dressed leaves on top. Add the anchovies, egg, and Parmesan, sprinkle with pepper, and serve with lemon wedges, if using.

couscous with feta, dill, and spring beans

1¾ cups couscous

1¾ cups boiling water

5 tablespoons extra virgin olive oil

1 garlic clove, crushed

3 shallots, peeled and thinly sliced

2 tablespoons freshly chopped dill

2 tablespoons freshly chopped chives

1 tablespoon finely chopped preserved lemon, or 1 tablespoon peel and flesh of fresh unwaxed lemon, finely chopped

8 oz. feta cheese, chopped

5 oz. sugar snap peas

5 oz. frozen fava broad beans, defrosted

5 oz. frozen peas, defrosted

freshly ground black pepper

SERVES 4

Dill is a herb that has never been terribly fashionable, unlike its peers, rosemary and sage. It's quite a floral, grassy herb and a whiff of it conjures up springtime, which is possibly why it is so well complemented by the beans and peas in this dish. Marinating the feta lifts it from a salty, creamy cheese to something much more complex, so it's well worth it, even if it's just for 5 minutes.

Put the couscous in a large bowl and pour over the boiling water. Cover with plastic wrap or a plate and let swell for 10 minutes.

Pour the olive oil into a mixing bowl and add the garlic, shallots, dill, chives, and preserved or fresh lemon and lots of freshly ground black pepper—the coarser the better. Add the feta, turn in the oil, and set aside while you cook the beans.

Bring a medium saucepan of unsalted water to a boil. Add the sugar snap peas, bring back to a boil, and cook for 1 minute. Add the fava beans, bring back to a boil, and cook for 1 minute. Finally, add the peas and cook for 2 minutes. Drain.

Uncover the couscous, stir in the hot beans, transfer to bowls, and top with the feta, spooning over the flavored oil as you go. Stir well before serving.

couscous salad with mint and cilantro

¼ cup couscous

½ cup boiling chicken stock or water

6 sun-blushed tomatoes (see page 61) or 6 fresh cherry tomatoes, halved

2 marinated artichoke hearts, well drained and halved

3–4 scallions, sliced

14 oz. canned chickpeas, drained and rinsed

HARISSA DRESSING

⅓ cup extra virgin olive oil

1 tablespoon sherry vinegar or cider vinegar

1 tablespoon harissa paste

sea salt and freshly ground black pepper

TO SERVE

a handful of fresh flatleaf parsley, coarsely chopped

watercress sprigs

fresh mint sprigs

cilantro sprigs

scissor-snipped fresh chives

SERVES 2

This very quick and easy salad is endlessly adaptable. Omit the chicken and add other uncooked or lightly blanched vegetables, such as cucumber, baby carrots, cherry tomatoes, sugar snap peas, asparagus tips, or herbs. Easy-cook couscous is supposed to be just soaked then drained, but it's often better if it's microwaved or steamed after soaking. It should be dry and fluffy.

Put the couscous in a heatproof bowl and cover with the stock or water. Leave for 15 minutes until the water has been absorbed. For a fluffier texture, put the soaked couscous in a strainer and steam over simmering water for another 10 minutes, or microwave in the bowl on 50 percent for about 5 minutes. Drain if necessary, pressing the liquid through the strainer with a spoon, then fluff up with a fork. Let cool.

Put the couscous in a bowl, add the tomatoes, artichoke hearts, scallions, and chickpeas. Keep the watercress and herbs in a separate container until just before serving.

To make the dressing, put the olive oil, vinegar, and harissa paste in a bowl and beat with a fork. Season to taste. Sprinkle half the dressing over the couscous mixture and toss with a fork. Add the watercress and herbs and serve. Serve the extra dressing separately.

Variation This is a perfect picnic, lunchbox, or make-ahead salad. Put the watercress and herbs into a small container and seal. Put the dressing ingredients in a screw-top jar, and shake to mix. Shake again just before serving. Put the couscous and remaining ingredients in a lidded plastic bowl, and seal until ready to use. To serve, add the dressing, parsley, and watercress and toss well.

chicken, apple, and peanut salad

2 apples, cored and chopped

1 tablespoon freshly squeezed lemon juice

2 cups baby spinach leaves, lightly rinsed

10 oz. grilled chicken breast, chopped

1 tablespoon unsalted roasted peanuts

4 tomatoes, chopped

½ small cucumber, chopped

2 tablespoons balsamic vinegar

sea salt and freshly ground black pepper

1 lemon, cut into wedges, to serve (optional)

SERVES 4

Peanuts are nutritional powerhouses. Not only do they provide you with eight vitamins and 13 minerals—including some that are hard to find naturally, such as magnesium and zinc—they contain plant chemicals which can help to protect against cancer. So this is an incredibly health-giving lunchtime salad!

Put the apples in a bowl, sprinkle with the lemon juice, and toss to coat. Add the spinach, chicken, peanuts, tomatoes, and cucumber.

Pour the balsamic vinegar over the salad, season, and toss well. Serve with lemon wedges, if using.

Variation This salad also tastes great with flaked smoked mackerel fillets instead of the chicken.

½ cup small pasta shapes

2 tablespoons pitted black or green olives or 2 tablespoons cooked corn

2 inches cucumber, roughly chopped

5 cherry tomatoes, halved

6 oz. canned tuna, drained and flaked

a few fresh chives, scissor-snipped

OLIVE OIL DRESSING

2 tablespoons olive oil

1 tablespoon freshly squeezed lemon juice

½ teaspoon Dijon or mild mustard

a pinch of salt

a pinch of freshly ground black pepper

SERVES 2

Small shell or "bow-tie" pasta works best here. The dressing is a tangy lemon and olive oil, and you could use cooked corn instead of the olives.

tuna pasta salad

Cook the pasta in salted boiling water according to the package instructions.

Drain the pasta in a colander and rinse it under cold water so it cools quickly and rinses off the starch. Let drain thoroughly in the colander while you make the rest of the salad.

Put the olives, cucumber, tomatoes, tuna, and chives in a bowl.

Put all the ingredients for the dressing in a screw-top jar and shake well. Season to taste.

Pour the dressing over the salad, then mix everything very gently with a metal spoon. Cover tightly and store in the refrigerator for up to 48 hours.

Most people love noodles, and the delicate spiciness in this recipe should not overpower sensitive taste buds. However, you can seed the chiles if you prefer a milder flavor. Make this quick, tasty recipe for a weekday dinner, then take the leftovers into work for a satisfying lunch the next day.

thai chicken noodle salad

1 tablespoon vegetable oil

12 oz. chicken breast, thinly sliced

½ inch fresh ginger, peeled and chopped

2 garlic cloves, crushed

1 lemon grass stalk, thinly sliced

1 medium–hot red or green chile, finely diced

10 oz. thick noodles

3 oz. bok choy, chopped

4 lime wedges, to serve

SERVES 4

Heat the vegetable oil in a wok or large skillet, add the chicken, ginger, garlic, lemon grass, and chile, and stir well. Cook over medium heat for 5 minutes, or until the chicken is cooked through and the lemon grass has softened.

Meanwhile, cook the noodles according to the package instructions, then drain.

Add the bok choy and cooked noodles to the wok and toss well. Serve with wedges of lime.

turkey cobb salad

4 fatty bacon slices

2 Hass avocados

1 large Bibb or Boston lettuce

6 ripe plum tomatoes, cut into wedges

1 lb. cooked turkey, shredded, at room temperature

2 hard-cooked eggs, quartered

4 oz. Roquefort cheese, cut into thin slices, or crumbled

olive oil, for cooking

LEMON CREAM DRESSING

1 cup heavy cream

freshly squeezed juice of 1 lemon

a handful of fresh chives, scissor-snipped

TO SERVE

crusty rolls

small cornichons, halved lengthwise, or sliced pickles

SERVES 4

This American classic was invented in the Roaring Twenties by a Californian restaurateur named Cobb. It's essentially a "bitser" salad—bitser this and bitser that—just like Niçoise or Gado Gado, two other legendary mixed salads. It's also a good post-turkey dish, when you have lots of turkey left over and you're looking for an effortless way to serve it. Traditionally, the ingredients were arranged in lines but this version is jumbled together. The dressing is a lighter, fresher take on the customary mayonnaise.

Brush a skillet with olive oil, add the bacon, and cook until crispy but not crumbly. Remove and drain on a crumpled paper towel.

Cut the avocados in half, remove the pits, then scoop out the flesh with a teaspoon.

Share the bacon, lettuce, tomatoes, turkey, eggs, cheese, and avocado between 4 plates or bowls.

To make the dressing, put the cream in a bowl, add the lemon juice, and beat well. Stir in the chives, then spoon over the salad and serve with crusty rolls and cornichons.

ENTRÉES

tagine of butternut squash, shallots, raisins, and almonds

3 tablespoons olive oil with a pat of butter

about 12 pink shallots, peeled and left whole

about 8 garlic cloves, lightly crushed

⅔ cup golden raisins

⅔ cup blanched almonds

1–2 teaspoons harissa paste

2 tablespoons dark honey

1 medium butternut squash, halved lengthwise, peeled, seeded, and sliced

sea salt and freshly ground black pepper

a small handful of cilantro, finely chopped, to serve

1 lemon, cut into wedges, to serve

SERVES 3–4

Substantial enough for a main meal, served with couscous and yogurt, vegetable tagines also make good side dishes for grilled or roasted meats or other tagines. You can cook this one in the oven if you like, using a tagine base or an ovenproof pan.

Heat the oil and butter in a tagine or heavy-based casserole dish. Stir in the shallots and garlic and sauté them until they begin to color. Add the raisins and almonds and stir in the harissa paste and honey. Toss in the squash, making sure it is coated in the spicy oil. Pour in enough water to cover the base of the tagine and cover with the lid. Cook gently for 15–20 minutes, until the shallots and squash are tender but still quite firm.

Season to taste, sprinkle the cilantro over the top, and serve with wedges of lemon to squeeze over the dish.

For nights when you want dinner in a hurry, this can be on the table in just 10 minutes. Serve with couscous or a mixture of basmati and wild rice, together with some green beans or cabbage.

½ small onion, sliced

⅔ cup vegetable stock

5 oz. mixed mushrooms, chopped if large

1 garlic clove, crushed

1 teaspoon whole-grain mustard

½ teaspoon tomato paste

1 tablespoon sour cream

sea salt and freshly ground black pepper

TO SERVE

freshly chopped parsley

couscous or a mixture of basmati and wild rice

green beans or cabbage

SERVES 1

mustardy mushroom stroganoff

Cook the onion in a covered saucepan with 3 tablespoons of the stock for about 4 minutes or until softened and the liquid has evaporated.

Stir in the mushrooms, garlic, and seasoning, then add the remaining stock, mustard, and tomato paste.

Cook, covered, for 2 minutes, then remove the lid and cook rapidly for 2 minutes to reduce the liquid to a syrup. Stir in the sour cream and parsley and serve immediately on a bed of couscous or rice, with green beans or cabbage on the side.

calabrian-style potatoes and bell peppers

⅔ cup olive oil

1 red bell pepper, halved, seeded, and thickly sliced

1 yellow bell pepper, halved, seeded, and thickly sliced

1¼ lb. Yukon gold potatoes, thinly sliced

sea salt and freshly ground black pepper

SERVES 4

This is a fine example of the "less is more" approach to cooking—simple, good-quality ingredients cooked to perfection.

Heat the olive oil in a large, lidded skillet. Add the red and yellow bell peppers and cook for 10 minutes, stirring occasionally, until starting to turn golden brown. Add the potatoes and some seasoning to the pan, cover with a lid, and cook for 5 minutes.

Remove the lid and continue cooking for 15 minutes, turning every few minutes as the potatoes begin to brown, taking care not to break them. If the potatoes start to stick, this will just add to the flavor of the dish, but don't let them burn.

When the potatoes are tender, transfer to a serving dish and let cool for 5 minutes before serving.

rice and bean burgers

1½ cups brown rice
(not parboiled variety)

2 tablespoons
Worcestershire sauce

1 onion, chopped

2 garlic cloves, crushed

6½ oz. canned cannellini beans,
drained and rinsed

6½ oz. canned red kidney beans,
drained and rinsed

½ cup fresh stoneground
whole-wheat bread crumbs

1 egg, beaten

4 oz. sharp cheddar cheese, grated

2 tablespoons freshly
chopped thyme

1 small green bell pepper,
seeded and chopped

1 large carrot, coarsely grated

whole-wheat flour or cornmeal,
for coating

2–3 tablespoons sunflower oil

sea salt and freshly ground
black pepper

TO SERVE

salad greens

relish

MAKES 10–12

There's something really satisfying about making your own burgers. These need to chill for 1½ hours so start them in advance. Pop any leftover burgers in the freezer before you cook them and take them out as and when you need them.

Cook the rice according to the package instructions, leaving it to overcook slightly so that it is soft. Drain the rice, transfer it to a large bowl, and reserve. Put 2 tablespoons water and the Worcestershire sauce in a skillet, add the onion and garlic, and cook over medium heat until softened, about 8 minutes.

Put the onion, garlic, cooked rice, beans, bread crumbs, egg, cheese, and thyme in a food processor. Add plenty of seasoning, then process until combined. Add the green bell pepper and grated carrot and mix well. Refrigerate for 1½ hours, or until quite firm.

Shape the mixture into 10–12 burgers, using wet hands if the mixture sticks. Coat them in flour or cornmeal and chill for a further 30 minutes. Preheat the oven to 375°F.

Put the burgers on a nonstick baking sheet and brush lightly with a little oil. Cook in the preheated oven for 20–25 minutes, or until piping hot. Alternatively, heat the oil in a nonstick sauté pan and fry the burgers for 3–4 minutes on each side, or until piping hot. Serve immediately with salad greens and relish.

Variation Add 1–2 seeded finely chopped chiles to give an extra bite and 3 finely chopped celery stalks to add some crunch.

cornmeal pizza tart

sea salt and freshly ground black pepper

leafy salad, to serve

PIZZA CRUST

1¾ cups vegetable stock

½ cup cornmeal, preferably stone-ground

2 tablespoons freshly grated Parmesan

PIZZA TOPPING

14 oz. canned chopped tomatoes

1 garlic clove, crushed

2 tablespoons freshly chopped basil

1 small zucchini, thinly sliced

½ red and ½ yellow bell pepper, seeded and thinly sliced

1 cup sliced mushrooms

½ small red onion, thinly sliced

1 teaspoon olive oil

2 oz. mozzarella cheese, sliced

1½ tablespoons finely grated Parmesan

a tart pan, 9 inches in diameter, lightly greased

SERVES 4

This has all the flavor of a pizza, but with a cornmeal crust instead of pizza dough. It makes the perfect no-fuss family dinner, which everyone will love.

Preheat the oven to 400°F.

Bring the stock to a boil in a large saucepan. Pour in the cornmeal in a steady stream and stir until bubbling. Reduce the heat and cook for 5 minutes, stirring occasionally, until thickened. Take care to protect your hand, as the bubbling cornmeal tends to spit. Remove from the heat and stir in the Parmesan and seasoning. Pour into the prepared tart pan and let cool and firm up for 10–15 minutes.

Tip the chopped tomatoes into a saucepan, add the garlic, basil, and seasoning and simmer briskly for 10 minutes until thickened. Spread over the cornmeal crust.

Mix the zucchini, bell peppers, mushrooms, and onion with the olive oil to coat, season lightly, and pile on top of the crust. Bake in the preheated oven for 10 minutes, then scatter the cheeses over the pizza tart. Return to the oven for 5 minutes, until the mozzarella starts to melt.

Cut into wedges and serve with a leafy salad.

3 tablespoons peanut or
safflower oil

1 onion, sliced

2 garlic cloves, chopped

1 inch fresh ginger,
peeled and grated

1 tablespoon hot red curry paste

1 teaspoon ground cinnamon

1 lb. potatoes, cubed

14 oz. canned chopped tomatoes

1¼ cups vegetable stock

1 tablespoon tomato paste

8 oz. button mushrooms, halved

8 oz. frozen peas

⅓ cup ground almonds

2 tablespoons freshly
chopped cilantro

sea salt and freshly ground
black pepper

basmati rice, to serve

SERVES 4

quick vegetable curry

This is a super-easy, quick, and tasty cheat's curry because it is made with ready-made curry paste. Serve with basmati rice.

Heat the oil in a saucepan and fry the onion, garlic, ginger, curry paste, and cinnamon for 5 minutes. Add the potatoes, tomatoes, stock, tomato paste, and some seasoning. Bring to a boil, cover, and simmer gently for 20 minutes.

Add the mushrooms, peas, ground almonds, and cilantro to the pan and cook for a further 10 minutes. Taste and adjust the seasoning if necessary. Serve with basmati rice.

Zucchini are so flavorful when cooked this way—bathed in garlic and olive oil, then stuffed with sweet, ripe cherry tomatoes and enveloped in melting fontina cheese. A delightfully fresh and summery dinner.

6 medium zucchini

2 garlic cloves, chopped

2 tablespoons olive oil, plus extra for sprinkling

about 30 cherry tomatoes, halved

3–4 tablespoons dried bread crumbs

8 oz. fontina cheese, sliced

sea salt and freshly ground black pepper

a shallow ovenproof dish, greased

SERVES 6

zucchini and tomatoes
baked with fontina

Preheat the oven to 325°F.

Halve the zucchini lengthwise and trim a little off the uncut sides so that they will sit still like boats. Using a teaspoon, scoop out the soft-seeded centers. Arrange the boats in a row in the prepared dish.

Put the garlic, olive oil, and some seasoning in a bowl, stir well, then brush over the cut surfaces of the zucchini. Arrange the halved tomatoes in the grooves. Season well, then sprinkle with olive oil and bread crumbs. Bake in the preheated oven for 30 minutes.

Remove from the oven and arrange the cheese over the zucchini and tomatoes. Return the dish to the oven for another 10 minutes to melt the cheese. Serve immediately while the cheese is still bubbling.

oven-roasted vegetables
with rosemary, bay leaves, and garlic

1 lb. boiling potatoes,
cut into 2-inch chunks

about 1 lb. butternut squash,
cut into wedges and seeded

6 small red onions, quartered

¼ cup extra virgin olive oil

8 garlic cloves (unpeeled)

2 red Cubanelle (long) peppers or
bell peppers, seeded and cut
into chunks

4 fresh rosemary sprigs

4 fresh bay leaf sprigs

sea salt

a large roasting pan

SERVES 4

Roasted vegetables are made extra special with the strong flavors of herbs. Thyme is good, but rosemary is even better (be sparing though—too much can overwhelm a dish). Bay leaves are quite mild when young, so don't use as many if you have mature leaves.

Preheat the oven to 400°F.

Bring a large saucepan of water to a boil, add salt and the potatoes, and cook for 5 minutes. Drain, then put in the roasting pan. Add the squash, onions, and 2 tablespoons of the oil. Toss to coat, then roast in the preheated oven for 10 minutes.

Add 1 extra tablespoon of oil to the roasting pan, followed by the garlic and peppers, 2 of the rosemary sprigs, and 2 of the bay sprigs. Roast for 15 minutes, then add the rest of the herbs and continue roasting for 10–15 minutes. Turn the vegetables occasionally until they are all tender and the edges slightly blackened. Trail the remaining oil over the top.

Variation Sprinkle with 3 tablespoons pine nuts and some crumbled feta cheese 5 minutes before the end of the cooking time, so the nuts roast a little and the feta softens.

Fresh or frozen spinach can be used in this recipe, but do make sure that both are thoroughly drained.

8 oz. macaroni

3 tablespoons butter

⅓ cup flour

2 cups milk

15 oz. cooked spinach, well drained

3 cups freshly grated Parmesan

sea salt and freshly ground black pepper

a large ovenproof dish

SERVES 4

macaroni, spinach, and cheese bake

Cook the macaroni according to the package instructions. Preheat the oven to 375°F.

Meanwhile, melt the butter in a saucepan, remove from the heat, and mix in the flour to make a *roux*. Return to a low heat and slowly pour in the milk, stirring constantly. Bring to a boil and cook for 1 minute, stirring frequently.

Drain the macaroni and add to the sauce along with the spinach, seasoning, and half the cheese. Mix well. Pour the mixture into the ovenproof dish, scatter the remaining cheese on top, and bake in the preheated oven for 15 minutes, until golden.

A simple and stylish pasta dish to cook at home, this traditional Italian recipe never seems to lose its appeal. Anchovies, either in oil or salted, are very good, as are tiny, compact capers. Buy them from a good Italian deli counter if you can. Both these ingredients are real gems that help make this piquant pantry dish just as memorable as it can be when eaten on holiday.

10 oz. spaghetti

4 tomatoes, peeled (see page 19), seeded, and chopped

1 cup pitted black olives

3 oz. canned anchovies, chopped

3 tablespoons capers

leaves from a large handful of fresh flatleaf parsley, chopped

¼ cup olive oil

freshly ground black pepper

¾ cup freshly grated Parmesan, to serve

SERVES 4

spaghetti puttanesca

Bring a large saucepan of water to a boil. Add the spaghetti, stir well to separate the strands, and simmer for 9 minutes.

When the spaghetti is cooked, drain it thoroughly. Dry the saucepan, then return the spaghetti to the pan, and add the tomatoes, olives, anchovies, capers, parsley, and olive oil. Season with pepper.

Toss the pasta well and serve with a dish of freshly grated Parmesan for sprinkling.

cannelloni with ricotta, bitter greens, and cherry tomato sauce

12 dried cannelloni tubes or
12 sheets fresh or dried lasagne

TOMATO SAUCE

3 tablespoons olive oil

2 garlic cloves, finely chopped

1½ lb. cherry tomatoes, halved

3 tablespoons freshly chopped basil

sea salt and freshly ground
black pepper

RICOTTA FILLING

3 oz. bitter salad greens, such as
arugula, watercress, or spinach

2 cups ricotta cheese

2 eggs, beaten

1 cup freshly grated Parmesan

freshly grated nutmeg, to taste

a pastry bag with a large round tip

a shallow ovenproof dish, greased

SERVES 4–6

This version of cannelloni combines a creamy sharp ricotta filling speckled with slightly bitter greens and a sweet tomato sauce. The contrast between the sauce and filling is amazing. The greens used here are easily available—arugula, watercress, or spinach.

Preheat the oven to 400°F.

To make the tomato sauce, heat the oil in a saucepan, add the garlic, and cook until just turning golden. Add the halved tomatoes. They should hiss as they go in—this will slightly caramelize the juices, and concentrate the flavor. Stir well, then simmer for 10 minutes. Stir in the basil and season (the sauce should still be quite lumpy). Set aside.

To make the ricotta filling, plunge the salad greens into a saucepan of boiling water for 1 minute, then drain well, squeezing out any excess moisture. Chop finely. Press the ricotta through a fine-mesh sieve into a bowl. Beat in the eggs, then add the chopped greens and half the Parmesan. Season with nutmeg, salt, and pepper. Set aside.

Cook the cannelloni or lasagne sheets in a large saucepan of salted boiling water according to the package instructions. Lift out of the water and drain on a clean dish towel.

Spoon the ricotta filling into the pastry bag. Fill each tube of cannelloni or pipe down the shorter edge of each lasagne sheet and roll it up. Arrange the filled cannelloni tightly together in a single layer in the prepared dish. Spoon over the tomato sauce and sprinkle with the remaining Parmesan. Bake in the preheated oven for 25–30 minutes until bubbling. Serve immediately.

pasta with fresh tomato

2 lb. ripe tomatoes

⅓ cup extra virgin olive oil

2 red chiles, seeded and chopped

2 garlic cloves, crushed

a bunch of fresh basil, chopped

1 teaspoon sugar

12 oz. spaghetti

cracked black pepper

freshly grated Pecorino Sardo or
Parmesan, to serve

SERVES 4

This sauce is best made as soon as the new season's tomatoes arrive in the shops, especially the vine-ripened varieties that we see more and more. Use the instructions on page 19 for an easy way to peel the tomatoes.

Peel the tomatoes according to the instructions on page 19, then put into a bowl. Add the oil, chiles, garlic, basil, sugar, and seasoning and let infuse while you cook the pasta (or longer if possible).

Cook the pasta according to the package instructions. Drain well and immediately stir in the fresh tomato sauce. Serve at once with the grated Parmesan.

This is a great mid-week dinner dish and just as good if people are coming over. It's also nice to have a change from tomato-based sauces. Pancetta is reasonably easy to find so do use that rather than bacon—pancetta is not as smoky and strong and its subtlety is just what's needed here.

2 cups shelled peas, fresh or frozen and defrosted

3–5 tablespoons extra virgin olive oil

⅓ cup fresh bread crumbs

16 oz. linguine

3 oz. thinly sliced pancetta, chopped

3 garlic cloves, crushed

a few fresh sage sprigs, leaves finely chopped

⅓ cup dry white wine

¼ cup freshly grated Parmesan

a small handful of fresh flatleaf parsley, chopped

fine sea salt and freshly ground black pepper

SERVES 4–6

linguine with peas, pancetta, and sage

Lightly blanch the peas in a pan of boiling water for 2–3 minutes. Drain and set aside.

Heat 2 tablespoons of the oil in a skillet. Add the bread crumbs and cook until toasted, stirring occasionally, about 3 minutes. Season lightly and set aside.

Cook the pasta in a large saucepan of salted boiling water according to the package instructions.

Heat the remaining oil in a saucepan large enough to hold all the pasta later. Add the pancetta and cook, stirring, until brown, about 2 minutes. Add the garlic and cook, stirring for 1 minute; don't let the garlic burn. Stir in the sage and wine. Cook, stirring until the liquid has almost evaporated, about 1 minute. Set aside until needed.

Drain the cooked pasta thoroughly and add to the pan of pancetta. Add the peas and 1–2 tablespoons more oil and cook over low heat, tossing well to mix. Stir in the cheese, parsley, and pepper; taste and add more seasoning if necessary. Sprinkle with the bread crumbs.

In Italy, pork is often braised with milk, as it tenderizes the meat and the juices mingle with the milk to provide a sweet, meaty sauce. Rosemary is lovely with pork but you could use chopped sage— just add it earlier when you brown the pork.

rigatoni with pork and lemon ragu

2 tablespoons olive oil

14 oz. ground pork

1 onion, finely chopped

2 garlic cloves, thinly sliced

4 anchovy fillets in oil, drained

2 tablespoons fresh
rosemary leaves

finely grated peel and freshly
squeezed juice of 1 unwaxed lemon

12 oz. rigatoni

2 cups whole milk

²/₃ cup green olives,
pitted and chopped

¹/₃ cup heavy cream

a good grating of fresh nutmeg

¹/₄ cup Parmesan shavings,
plus extra to serve

sea salt and freshly ground
black pepper

SERVES 4

Put a large saucepan of salted water on to boil for the rigatoni.

Meanwhile, heat the olive oil in a large skillet over high heat and add the pork. Leave it for a few minutes until it browns, then turn it over and allow the other side to brown too. Add the onion, garlic, anchovies, rosemary, and lemon peel and stir to combine with the pork. Reduce the heat, cover, and let the onion soften for 10 minutes, stirring occasionally so the ingredients don't stick to the bottom of the skillet.

When the salted water in the large pan is boiling, add the rigatoni and cook according to the package instructions until al dente.

When the onion is translucent, add the milk, lemon juice, and olives, and bring to a boil, uncovered, scraping the base of the skillet to loosen any sticky, flavorful bits and incorporating them into the sauce. Simmer for about 15–20 minutes, or until about two-thirds of the liquid has evaporated and the pork is soft. Stir in the cream, then season with salt, pepper, and nutmeg.

Drain the rigatoni, put it back into its pan, and spoon in the pork ragu. Add the Parmesan shavings, stir well, and transfer to bowls. Sprinkle the extra Parmesan shavings on top.

This uncomplicated pomodoro sauce relies upon using the best canned Italian peeled plum tomatoes you can find. The milk-soaked bread and Parmesan keep the meatballs feather-light and impossible to stop eating.

spaghetti and meatballs

14 oz. ground pork or beef

1 small yellow onion, very finely chopped

1 egg, beaten

5 garlic cloves, finely chopped

3 tablespoons freshly chopped flatleaf parsley

3 tablespoons freshly grated Parmesan, plus extra to serve

1 teaspoon each salt and freshly ground pepper

2 slices of white bread

3 tablespoons milk

5 tablespoons olive oil

three 14-oz. cans whole, peeled plum tomatoes

1 tablespoon butter

14 oz. spaghetti

SERVES 4

Preheat the oven to 400°F.

Combine the pork, onion, egg, most of the garlic, parsley, Parmesan, and some seasoning. Put the bread in a separate bowl and pour over the milk. Break the mixture up into small pieces then add to the bowl with the meat. Mix everything with your hands until well combined. Roll into 2-inch balls and place on a baking sheet lined with parchment paper or aluminum foil. Bake in the preheated oven for 15 minutes, giving the meatballs a shake halfway through cooking so they don't stick. Set aside.

In a large, wide saucepan, heat the olive oil and cook the remaining garlic until golden but not brown. Add the tomatoes and break up with a flat spoon. Season. Cook over medium/high heat for 15 minutes, stirring every 5 minutes or so. Keep a splatter screen on while cooking. The sauce should be thick when it is done. Add the butter and the meatballs.

Boil the spaghetti in plenty of salted water until it is just al dente. Drain and mix with the sauce. Serve sprinkled with grated Parmesan.

This is a great way to use up leftover spaghetti. The spaghetti is mixed with fresh arrabbiata sauce made with tomatoes and chiles to add a fiery kick.

spaghetti and arugula frittata

3 tablespoons extra virgin olive oil

1 onion, chopped

1 garlic clove, crushed

3 ripe plum tomatoes, chopped

1 fresh red chile, seeded and finely chopped

2 tablespoons tomato paste

²/₃ cup white wine or water

2–2½ cups cold cooked spaghetti (5 oz. before cooking)

6 extra-large eggs

2 tablespoons freshly grated Parmesan

a small handful of arugula

2 tablespoons balsamic vinegar

sea salt and freshly ground black pepper

a 12-inch heavy nonstick skillet (measure the base, not the top)

SERVES 4

Heat 1 tablespoon of the oil in a saucepan, add the onion, and sauté for 5 minutes until softened. Add the garlic, tomatoes, and chile and cook for 3–4 minutes, stirring several times. Add the tomato paste and wine or water and simmer for 5 minutes. Remove from the heat, add the spaghetti, and toss gently.

Break the eggs into a large bowl and beat briefly with a fork. Add the spaghetti and sauce and mix gently.

Heat the remaining oil in the skillet, add the spaghetti and egg mixture, and cook over low heat for 10–12 minutes, or until golden brown on the underside and almost set on the top. Meanwhile, preheat the broiler.

Sprinkle with the Parmesan and slide under the preheated broiler for 30–60 seconds to melt the cheese and finish cooking the top. Let cool for 5 minutes, then transfer to a plate. Put the arugula on top of the frittata, sprinkle with balsamic vinegar, and serve.

There's something uniquely comforting about risotto. And when it's made with autumnal squash and woody sage, it becomes the perfect one-bowl meal to serve up on a cold, dark evening in front of the television. It tastes wonderful on its own or served with grilled lamb chops.

butternut squash, sage, and chile risotto

about 6 cups hot chicken or vegetable stock

1 stick unsalted butter

1 large onion, finely chopped

1–2 fresh or dried red chiles, seeded and finely chopped

1 lb. fresh butternut squash or pumpkin, peeled, seeded, and finely diced

2⅓ cups risotto rice

3 tablespoons freshly chopped sage

¾ cups freshly grated Parmesan

sea salt and freshly ground black pepper

SERVES 6

Pour the stock into a saucepan and keep at a gentle simmer. Melt half the butter in a large, heavy saucepan and add the onion. Cook gently for 10 minutes until soft, golden, and translucent but not brown. Stir in the chopped chiles and cook for 1 minute. Add the butternut or pumpkin and cook, stirring constantly, for 5 minutes, until it begins to soften slightly. Stir in the rice to coat with the butter and vegetables. Cook for a few minutes to toast the grains.

Begin adding the stock, a large ladle at a time, stirring gently until each ladle has almost been absorbed by the rice. The risotto should be barely simmering throughout cooking, so don't let the rice dry out—add more stock as necessary. Continue until the rice is tender and creamy, but the grains still firm and the squash beginning to disintegrate. (This should take 15–20 minutes depending on the type of rice used—check the package instructions.)

Season to taste and stir in the sage, remaining butter, and all the Parmesan. Cover, let rest for a couple of minutes, then serve.

Ideal for an indulgent lunch or dinner, this creamy rice cake oozes with mozzarella, and has pockets of tomatoes that burst with flavor. You could even add a layer of cubed mozzarella to the middle of the tart, so that the center exudes strings of melted cheese when you cut it.

three-colored rice and cheese cake

¼ cup cornmeal or dried bread crumbs

4 cups fresh or 8 oz. frozen whole leaf spinach, thawed

3 eggs, beaten

2 cups plus 2 tablespoons risotto rice (not long-grain)

1 tablespoon olive oil

2 tablespoons butter

1 onion, finely chopped

freshly grated nutmeg

8 oz. tiny cherry tomatoes

6 oz. mozzarella cheese, cubed

¼ cup freshly grated Parmesan

sea salt and freshly ground black pepper

an 8-inch nonstick springform cake pan, heavily greased

SERVES 6

Preheat the oven to 400°F. Dust the prepared cake pan with the cornmeal or dried bread crumbs.

If using fresh spinach, tear off the stems. Wash the leaves well, then put them, still wet, in a covered saucepan and cook for a few minutes until wilted. Drain well but do not squeeze dry—you want large pieces of spinach. If using thawed spinach, lightly squeeze it to remove excess moisture and toss the leaves a little to loosen them. Mix the spinach into the beaten eggs.

Cook the rice in a large saucepan of salted boiling water for about 10 minutes, until almost tender, then drain. Heat the oil and butter in a skillet. Add the onion and cook until golden. Stir into the rice.

Season the egg and spinach mixture with nutmeg, salt, and pepper. Stir into the rice, then fold in the cherry tomatoes, cubed mozzarella, and Parmesan. Spoon into the prepared cake pan and level the surface.

Bake in the preheated oven for 25–30 minutes, until firm and golden. Turn out and serve hot, cut into wedges.

chicken and barley supper

Healthy, wholesome, and satisfying, this is the kind of meal that needs plenty of time on the stove to become really tasty and tender. In the meantime, you can put your feet up and relax.

2 tablespoons whole-wheat flour

1 lb. skinless, boneless chicken breasts, cubed

3½ oz. lean bacon slices, cut into strips

2 medium onions, chopped

2 carrots, sliced

2 celery stalks, chopped

3–4 cups white wine or chicken stock

3 tablespoons pearl barley, rinsed

1 tablespoon freshly chopped mixed herbs, such as rosemary, basil, parsley, and thyme, plus extra to serve

freshly ground black pepper

SERVES 4

Season the flour with black pepper, then toss the chicken cubes in the flour. Heat a large nonstick skillet or saucepan, add the bacon, and dry-fry for 5 minutes, stirring frequently, until the fat starts to run. Add the chicken and sauté for 5–8 minutes, turning frequently, until the chicken is sealed all over. Remove the chicken and bacon from the skillet with a slotted spoon and set aside.

Add the onion, carrots, celery, and ¼ cup of the wine or stock to the skillet and sauté for 5 minutes, until the vegetables are softened. Add the pearl barley, herbs, and 2½ cups of the wine or stock. Bring to a boil, then cover, reduce the heat, and simmer for 1 hour. Add more wine or stock as it is absorbed.

Return the chicken and bacon to the skillet and continue to simmer for a further 30 minutes, or until the pearl barley and chicken are tender. Stir occasionally during cooking, adding a little more wine or stock, if necessary. Serve sprinkled with more chopped herbs and accompanied by a selection of your favorite vegetables.

Variation Use half the amount of chicken and cook as above. Once all the ingredients are tender, use a slotted spoon to remove 2–3 tablespoons of the mixture and reserve. Put the remainder in a food processor and blend to form a purée. Return to a clean saucepan together with the reserved ingredients. Heat until piping hot, adding a little extra stock or water to make a warming winter soup. You could do the same with any leftovers, taking care when reheating to make sure that it is piping hot.

There is a wonderful fragrance to Thai curries, and they make a fantastic family meal. Build up the chile content gradually until you find a spiciness that everyone enjoys. Plain jasmine rice is a good accompaniment.

thai green curry

2 tablespoons vegetable oil

1 onion, sliced

2 inches fresh ginger, peeled and sliced

2 garlic cloves, crushed

1 lemon grass stalk, chopped

1 mild green chile, diced

4 chicken breast fillets, sliced

2 kaffir lime leaves

2 tablespoons Thai green curry paste

¾ cup coconut milk

freshly squeezed juice of 1 lime

½ cup broccoli florets

½ cup green beans, trimmed

sea salt and freshly ground black pepper

jasmine rice, to serve

SERVES 4

Heat the oil in a large saucepan, add the onion, ginger, garlic, lemon grass, and chile, and cook over low heat for 5 minutes. Add the chicken and cook for a further 5 minutes.

Add the kaffir lime leaves and curry paste and mix well. Shake the tin of coconut milk and slowly pour into the curry, mixing constantly. Pour in ⅓ cup water and the lime juice, bring to a simmer, and cook gently for 5 minutes. Add the broccoli and beans and simmer for another 3 minutes. Serve with boiled jasmine rice.

chicken and bacon pot

1 tablespoon olive oil

10 oz. thick bacon, diced

8 oz. button mushrooms

4 chicken breast fillets

1 garlic clove, crushed

2 shallots, diced

⅓ cup flour

2 cups chicken stock

1 cup white wine

1 bay leaf

a handful of fresh parsley, chopped

sea salt and freshly ground black pepper

a mixture of basmati and wild rice, to serve

SERVES 4

The bacon add a special intensity to the flavor of this easy-to-make dish. Serve with rice to mop up the lovely sauce.

Preheat the oven to 350°F.

Heat the olive oil in a casserole dish, add the bacon and mushrooms, and cook over medium heat until golden. Transfer to a plate.

Put the chicken breasts in the casserole and quickly brown on both sides. Set aside with the bacon.

Sauté the garlic and shallots over low heat in the same pan for 5 minutes. Add the flour and mix well. Remove the pan from the heat, slowly pour in the stock and wine, and stir until smooth. Return to the heat and bring to a boil, stirring constantly. Mix in the bacon and mushrooms, then add the chicken, bay leaf, and seasoning. Cover and cook in the oven for 30 minutes. Add the parsley just before serving with rice.

This is a popular cold salad and a tasty way to use up leftover roast chicken. The creamy peanut butter dressing sets it apart from other salads.

bang bang chicken

14 oz. ready–cooked boneless chicken, such as smoked chicken, cold roast chicken, or cold turkey

1 large carrot

salad leaves, such as crisp lettuce or Chinese leaves, about 1 cup

1 medium cucumber, cut into strips

BANG BANG DRESSING

5 tablespoons crunchy peanut butter

1 scallion, very thinly sliced

1 teaspoon sesame oil

1 teaspoon soy sauce

1 teaspoon sugar

1 teaspoon Chinese white rice vinegar or cider vinegar

1 teaspoon rice wine or water

3 tablespoons hot water

SERVES 4

Remove any skin from the chicken and discard. Pull or cut the chicken into shreds. Shred the carrot with a vegetable peeler to make ultra-thin long ribbons.

Tear any large salad leaves into bite-size pieces. Arrange the leaves on a serving dish. Scatter the cucumber sticks and carrot ribbons over the leaves. Arrange the chicken on the top.

To make the dressing, put the peanut butter, scallion, sesame oil, soy sauce, sugar, vinegar, rice wine or water, and hot water to the bowl. Stir gently until well mixed. Taste the dressing—it should be a harmonious balance of salty, sweet, and sour flavors, so add more vinegar, sugar, or soy as you think is needed. The dressing should be just thin enough to spoon over the chicken, so if it is too thick stir in another tablespoon or so of hot water.

When the sauce seems perfect, spoon it over the chicken and serve.

Mildly spicy and full of flavor, these chicken balls are made with your hands, then simply baked in the oven—no frying needed. Serve with Thai fragrant rice and extra sweet chili sauce for dipping. Super easy and super delicious.

thai meatballs with chicken

2 oz. fresh bread crumbs

1 lb. ground chicken or turkey

1 egg

2 scallions, very thinly sliced

½ teaspoon ground coriander

a small handful of cilantro leaves, chopped

1 teaspoon fish sauce or soy sauce

2 teaspoons sweet chili sauce, plus extra for serving

Thai fragrant rice, to serve

a large baking dish, oiled

MAKES 12

Preheat the oven to 400°F.

Put the bread crumbs, chicken or turkey, egg, scallions, ground coriander, cilantro, fish sauce or soy sauce, and chili sauce in a bowl.

Mix well with your hands, then roll the mixture into small balls—use about 1 tablespoon of mixture for each.

Arrange the meatballs in the prepared baking dish. Bake in the preheated oven for 25 minutes until golden brown and cooked all the way through.

Serve the meatballs straight from the baking dish with some sweet chili sauce for dipping and some Thai fragrant rice on the side.

This gorgeous, tangy dish can be prepared in advance up to the point where it is put in the oven. The sauce around the duck, before it is put into the oven, must be very thick, because the bok choy or cabbage gives off so much water that the dish can easily become diluted.

braised duck and ginger

4 large duck breasts, cut into thick slices

5 teaspoons cornstarch

4 tablespoons yellow bean paste or sauce

2 tablespoons Shao Xing (sweet Chinese rice wine) or mirin

2 teaspoons sugar

freshly ground black pepper

1 onion, finely chopped

2 tablespoons peanut oil

4 inches fresh ginger, peeled and thickly sliced

2 garlic cloves, crushed

grated peel of 1 unwaxed orange or tangerine

2 tablespoons dark soy sauce

4 baby bok choy, halved lengthwise or ½ Chinese cabbage, sliced crosswise

SERVES 4

Preheat the oven to 350°F.

Put the duck in a bowl, sprinkle with 1 teaspoon of the cornstarch, and mix until coated.

Heat a wok or skillet, add the duck, and stir-fry to release the fat and firm up the meat. Remove with a slotted spoon and return the duck to the bowl.

Put the bean paste or sauce in a small bowl, add ½ cup water, the Shao Xing or mirin, sugar, and freshly ground black pepper, and mix well.

Add the onion to the wok or skillet, then add the bean paste mixture. Simmer for about 30 seconds, then pour the mixture over the duck. Reheat the wok with the oil and sauté the ginger and garlic to release their flavor. Return the duck and its sauce to the wok, add the peel, and simmer lightly until most of the water has evaporated.

Mix the remaining cornstarch with 2 tablespoons water and the soy sauce, stir into the wok, and bring to a boil, stirring.

Line a heavy casserole dish with the bok choy or Chinese cabbage, arrange the duck over the top, then pour over the sauce. Cook in the preheated oven for 10 minutes until tender. Remove from the oven and, if the leaves have given off too much liquid, pour it into a saucepan or wok and boil until it thickens again to a coating consistency.

A healthy version of the Greek favorite, this is a good dish to prepare in advance. Eggplant contains a host of vitamins and minerals and provides the perfect receptacle for the simple moussaka filling.

2 eggplants

1 teaspoon olive oil

10 oz. ground lamb

1 onion, finely chopped

2 garlic cloves, crushed

1 teaspoon ground cinnamon

1 teaspoon dried mint

1 tablespoon tomato paste

salad, to serve

TOPPING

⅔ cup Greek (strained) yogurt

1 egg yolk

freshly grated nutmeg

2 tomatoes, sliced

SERVES 4

moussaka–filled eggplant

Preheat the broiler to medium.

Cut both eggplants in half lengthwise and scoop out the flesh with a spoon, leaving an inner shell approximately ¼ inch thick. Cut the eggplant flesh into small dice and set aside for the filling. Rub the olive oil into the eggplant shells and season the flesh lightly, then put under the preheated broiler for 5–6 minutes until golden brown and slightly softened. Transfer to a baking sheet.

Preheat the oven to 400°F.

Put the ground lamb into a nonstick skillet. Dry-fry with the onion and garlic over high heat for 5 minutes until brown. Mix in the eggplant flesh, cinnamon, mint, tomato paste, and 6 tablespoons cold water, season the mixture, and cook for 5 minutes.

Spoon the lamb filling into the eggplant shells. Mix the yogurt with the egg yolk, nutmeg, and seasoning, then pour this over the filling. Top with the sliced tomatoes and bake in the preheated oven for 20 minutes. Serve with a salad.

This is very simple but surprisingly effective, given how few ingredients there are, so make sure you adjust the seasoning carefully as it makes such a difference. Trim the stem end only of the okra, taking off the tiniest layer of the already-cut surface, to discourage the sticky liquid from oozing out.

greek braised lamb
with okra

3 tablespoons olive oil

4 lamb steaks, about 2 lb., cut from the leg and deboned

1 small onion, sliced

2 garlic cloves, crushed

4 tomatoes, peeled (see page 19) and seeded

8 oz. okra, trimmed

sea salt and freshly ground black pepper

new potatoes, to serve

freshly chopped flatleaf parsley, to serve

SERVES 4

Preheat the oven to 350°F.

Heat the oil in a wide, shallow, flameproof casserole dish or saucepan. Season the meat, add to the pan, and brown the pieces all over. Remove the meat with a slotted spoon, put on a plate, and set aside in a warm place.

Add the onion and garlic to the pan and cook until softened and slightly brown. Add the tomatoes and simmer to a pulp.

Return the lamb to the pan, turn to coat, taste and adjust the seasoning, and cover with a lid. Bring to a boil on top of the stove, then transfer to the preheated oven and simmer for 20 minutes.

Add the okra, cover, and simmer for a further 20 minutes, removing the lid for the last 10 minutes of cooking time, to let the liquid reduce enough to just coat the meat without becoming oily. Serve with new potatoes and sprinkle with chopped parsley.

Nothing beats a classic leg of lamb for a favorite family roast. At the weekend, when you can afford to spend a little more time cooking, this is a lovely meal to prepare to get the whole family sitting round the dinner table together. Try this Italian take on the classic version—flavored with lemon and garlic, with the salty seasoning in the gravy supplied by anchovies.

italian roast leg of lamb
with lemon and anchovy sauce

1 leg of lamb, about 6 lb.

2 garlic cloves, thinly sliced

1 tablespoon olive oil

¾ cup white wine

sea salt and freshly ground black pepper

SAUCE

5 anchovy fillets

¾ cup chicken stock

grated lemon peel from 1 unwaxed lemon

1 tablespoon freshly chopped flatleaf parsley

an instant-read thermometer

SERVES 5

Preheat the oven to 400°F if you want the lamb medium rare, or 325°F for well done.

Make slits in the meat in several places and insert the slivers of garlic. Brush the lamb with the oil and season all over. Set it in a roasting pan and pour the wine around. Roast in the preheated oven until an instant-read thermometer registers 145°F for medium rare, or until the thermometer registers 170°F for well done. It will take 1¼–2½ hours depending on the oven temperature. Baste the meat from time to time, adding water if the wine becomes low.

When the lamb is cooked to your liking, transfer it to a serving dish and let rest in a warm place while you make the gravy. Discard any excess fat from the roasting pan, then add the anchovies, crushing them to a paste with a fork. Stir in the stock until the anchovies have been absorbed. Add the lemon peel and parsley and any juices that have come out of the lamb during the resting period, then pour into a sauceboat to serve.

1 medium onion, coarsely chopped

4 garlic cloves, coarsely chopped

1 red bell pepper, halved,
seeded, and coarsely chopped

1 fresh fat red chile,
seeded and chopped

2 teaspoons mild chili seasoning (powder)

1 teaspoon sweet paprika

1 teaspoon ground cumin

1 teaspoon ground coriander

½ teaspoon ground cinnamon

1 teaspoon dried oregano

1¼ cups lager beer

1 lb. pork steak

¼ cup safflower oil

14 oz. canned chopped tomatoes

1½ cups tomato juice or passata

1 oz. very dark chocolate, chopped

14 oz. canned pinto beans or
black-eyed peas, drained and rinsed

sea salt and freshly ground
black pepper

TO SERVE

soft tortillas

tomato salsa

chopped avocado in sour cream

green rice

SERVES 4–6

mexican pork and beans
in red chile sauce

This special version of chili is made with pork and just a few beans, then enriched Mexican-style with a little chocolate for depth. Don't be put off by the list of ingredients. You will already have many of them in your kitchen cupboards. Serve it with salsa, chopped avocado in sour cream, warm tortillas, and plenty of green rice (basmati steamed with herbs and spinach) for a great family feast. It's even better made the day before and it freezes very well.

Put the onion, garlic, bell pepper, chile, chili seasoning, paprika, cumin, coriander, cinnamon, and oregano in a food processor. Add half the lager and blend to a smooth purée.

Trim the pork steaks, then cut into large pieces. Working in batches, heat the oil in a large saucepan, add the pork, and fry until brown. Transfer to a plate.

Add the purée to the pan and cook, stirring continuously, over moderate heat for 5 minutes—make sure it doesn't catch and burn, but it should start to caramelize. Stir in the remaining lager, tomatoes, tomato juice, the pork, and juices. Season and bring to a boil. Reduce the heat and simmer very gently, half-covered, for 30–35 minutes until the pork is tender and the sauce thickened. Stir in the chocolate and beans and heat through.

Serve with the tortillas, salsa, chopped avocado in sour cream, and green rice.

pork with leeks and mushroom sauce

two lean pork loin steaks,
4 oz. each

½ teaspoon olive oil

1 leek, chopped

3½ oz. mushrooms, sliced

⅓ cup chicken stock

2 teaspoons whole-grain mustard

1 teaspoon cornstarch blended
with a little cold water

2 tablespoons sour cream

sea salt and freshly ground
black pepper

roasted squash, to serve

SERVES 2

The satisfying savory sauce is a fabulous complement to pork and it really couldn't be easier to throw together. The dish goes particularly well with roasted squash.

Lightly season the pork steaks and heat the olive oil in a nonstick skillet. Add the pork and sauté for 4 minutes on one side, then turn, scattering the leeks around the pork. Cook for 2 minutes, then stir in the mushrooms and cook for 2 minutes. Remove the pork steaks to a plate to keep warm while you finish the sauce.

Pour the stock into the skillet, mix in the mustard, and boil rapidly for 3 minutes until slightly syrupy. Stir the blended cornstarch into the skillet and cook until the sauce has thickened slightly. Remove from the heat and stir in the sour cream. Spoon the sauce over the pork steaks and serve accompanied by roasted squash.

herby sausages with polenta
and rosemary, red onion, and red currant gravy

8 herb-flavor sausages

sea salt and freshly ground
black pepper

**ROSEMARY, RED ONION, AND
RED CURRANT GRAVY**

2 tablespoons olive oil

2 red onions, thinly sliced

2 fresh rosemary sprigs, broken up

2 teaspoons flour

2 tablespoons red currant jelly

1¼ cups red wine

1¼ cups beef stock

2 tablespoons butter

POLENTA

1 cup fine cornmeal

3½ tablespoons butter

¾ cup freshly grated Parmesan

SERVES 4

This is an Italian take on sausages and mashed potatoes but with a bit of British red currant jelly thrown in because it makes onion gravy sticky. If you've tried polenta (cornmeal) before and weren't blown away, try it again now: the secret, as with most of the good things in life, is lots of butter, cheese, and seasoning.

Put 3 cups water in a medium pan over high heat, cover, and heat until it simmers.

Pour the cornmeal into the pan of simmering water and beat out any lumps. Reduce the heat to low and bubble away for 30 minutes or according to the package instructions.

To make the rosemary, red onion, and red currant gravy, heat the olive oil in a skillet and start cooking the onions and rosemary over medium heat, stirring. When the onions are beginning to soften, reduce the heat, cover, and let soften slowly in their own juices. After 10–15 minutes, stir in the flour and cook for about 1 minute until it is no longer pale. Add the jelly, wine, and stock and bring to a boil. Let bubble away gently for 15 minutes while you cook the sausages.

Preheat the broiler. Put the sausages on a baking sheet lined with aluminum foil and broil for 15 minutes, turning halfway through.

When everything is ready, beat the butter and Parmesan into the cornmeal and season. Beat the butter into the gravy and season to taste. Transfer the polenta to bowls, top with 2 sausages, and pour over the hot gravy.

Spareribs make a wonderful dinner, because they can be cooked in advance and reheated when required. Amazingly, when roasted in the oven, they are more succulent than they are when grilled (the usual method). Because they are cooked long and slowly, they don't dry out so much.

roast sticky spareribs
marinated and glazed

4 lb. spareribs

STICKY MARINADE

2 tablespoons honey

¼ **cup soy sauce**

1 tablespoon ground ginger

1 tablespoon Dijon mustard

1 tablespoon grated fresh ginger

1 teaspoon oil

SERVES 4

To make the marinade, put the honey, soy sauce, ground ginger, mustard, fresh ginger, and oil in a roasting pan and mix well. Add the ribs and turn to coat with the mixture. Set aside for several hours or overnight in the refrigerator.

Remove the pan from the refrigerator about 30 minutes before you want to start cooking, so the ribs can return to room temperature while you preheat the oven. Preheat the oven to 350°F.

Roast in the preheated oven for 1½ hours, turning over after 1 hour. Serve with napkins.

This recipe makes a change from ordinary mashed potatoes. Serve with roast chicken or pork and the meal is pretty much complete. Alternatively, this is useful when cooking for a mixed crowd of carnivores and vegetarians. Omit the ham and it can serve as a vegetarian entrée.

mashed potato pie with
peas, ham, cheese, and chives

2 lb. potatoes

1 bay leaf

1 tablespoon extra virgin olive oil

1 onion, finely chopped

1 cup shelled peas, fresh or frozen and thawed

2 tablespoons unsalted butter

1 cup milk or cream (or a bit of both)

1 egg, beaten

2 oz. ham, sliced into thin ribbons

a small bunch of fresh chives, scissor-snipped

1 cup grated sharp cheddar cheese

sea salt and freshly ground black pepper

a baking dish or ceramic tart mold, 10 inches in diameter, well greased

SERVES 4

Preheat the oven to 375°F.

Peel the potatoes and halve if large (the potatoes should all be about the same size to cook evenly). Put in a large saucepan, add water to cover, then add the bay leaf and some salt. Boil until tender, about 20 minutes.

Meanwhile, heat the oil in a skillet, add the onion and a pinch of salt, and fry until brown, about 5–7 minutes. Put the peas in a microwave-proof bowl with water to cover and microwave on HIGH for 3 minutes, then drain. (Alternatively, blanch in boiling water for 3 minutes.)

Drain the cooked potatoes, then mash, mixing in the butter and milk or cream. Season with salt and stir in the egg until well blended.

Stir in the onion, peas, ham, chives, and half the cheddar. Season to taste. Transfer to the prepared dish and spread evenly. Sprinkle with the remaining cheddar and bake in the preheated oven until well browned, 40–45 minutes. Serve hot or warm.

This is a gentle, aromatic meat curry from Indonesia made all in one pot with cubed beef. Tamarind paste is sold in small jars in supermarkets and Asian stores. Serve with Thai fragrant rice and green beans.

beef rendang

1 lb. steak for stewing, cubed

1 tablespoon tamarind paste

1 cinnamon stick

1 tablespoon brown sugar

2 tablespoons soy sauce

1 cup unsalted beef or vegetable stock

¼ teaspoon ground black pepper

¼ teaspoon freshly grated nutmeg

seeds from 6 cardamom pods, crushed

2 medium red onions, quartered

3 garlic cloves, roughly chopped

1 inch fresh ginger, peeled and roughly chopped

Thai fragrant rice, to serve

green beans, to serve

SERVES 4

Put the meat in a heavy medium saucepan or casserole dish. Add the tamarind, cinnamon stick, sugar, soy sauce, stock, pepper, nutmeg, and cardamom seeds.

Put the onions, garlic, and ginger in a food processor and blend until very finely chopped. Spoon into the saucepan with the rest of the ingredients and set over medium heat. Bring the mixture to a boil, stir gently to make sure everything is well combined, then cover with a lid.

Turn the heat right down and let simmer very gently for 1½ hours, stirring now and then. Remove the lid and cook uncovered for a further 20–30 minutes until the sauce is very thick. Remove the cinnamon stick and serve.

homemade burgers

20 oz. lean ground beef

1 garlic clove, crushed

1 shallot, finely diced

a handful of fresh parsley, chopped

1 teaspoon Worcestershire sauce

olive oil, for frying

4 fatty bacon slices

4 small ciabatta loaves

4 tablespoons mayonnaise

4 slices of beef tomato

1 cup grated sharp cheddar cheese (optional)

1 avocado, sliced

4 iceberg lettuce leaves, shredded

sea salt and freshly ground black pepper

ketchup and mustard, to serve

MAKES 4

Burgers are fantastically versatile, so build yours just as you wish, with or without the garnishes suggested below.

Preheat the broiler to medium.

Put the ground beef, garlic, shallot, parsley, and Worcestershire sauce in a large bowl, season, and mix well with your hands. Divide the mixture into 4 and shape into burgers.

Heat some oil in a large skillet and cook the burgers for 2 minutes on each side for rare, 3 minutes for medium-rare, and 4 minutes for well done.

Meanwhile, broil the bacon under the preheated broiler until crisp. Cut the ciabatta loaves in half and broil the insides, then spread with mayonnaise. Put a slice of tomato on the broiled base and a burger on top, followed by a handful of cheddar, if using, a bacon slice, a slice or two of avocado, and some lettuce. Sandwich together with the remaining bread and serve with ketchup and mustard.

Steak and melting, gooey blue cheese are a match made in heaven. This recipe uses mature Stilton, but you could equally well use Gorgonzola.

toasted steak, stilton, and watercress sandwich

2 oz. mature blue Stilton, rind removed

2 tablespoons butter, softened

a small pinch of cayenne pepper or paprika

two 8-oz. thinly sliced bottom round steaks

1 tablespoon olive oil

1 medium ciabatta loaf

a small handful of watercress

sea salt and freshly ground black pepper

BALSAMIC DRESSING

1 teaspoon balsamic vinegar

3 teaspoons light olive oil

a ridged stovetop grill pan (optional)

SERVES 2

Preheat the broiler to hot.

To make the balsamic dressing, mix the vinegar and olive oil and some seasoning in a small bowl. Set aside.

Mash the Stilton with the butter and season with the cayenne pepper. Heat a ridged stovetop grill pan or a skillet over high heat until very hot. Rub the slices of steak lightly with the olive oil and season. Sear for 1 minute each side, then set aside.

Cut the ciabatta in half crosswise, then in half lengthwise. Briefly toast the outside of the bottom halves under the preheated broiler, then turn them over and pile on the steak slices and dot with the Stilton butter. Broil for about 1 minute until the cheese melts, then transfer to warm plates.

Lightly toast the outside of the remaining halves of ciabatta. Place a few watercress leaves on top of the Stilton butter and drizzle with the balsamic dressing, then cover with the remaining ciabatta halves. Serve immediately.

a fabulous paella

3 tablespoons good olive oil

6 chicken thighs

6 oz. chorizo, cut into chunks

2 garlic cloves, finely chopped

1 large onion, finely chopped

1 large red bell pepper, seeded and finely sliced

2½ cups Spanish paella rice

¾ cup dry white wine

a good pinch of dried hot pepper flakes

2 teaspoons sweet Spanish paprika

about 5 cups chicken stock

a large pinch of saffron threads, soaked in 3 tablespoons hot water

6 ripe tomatoes, quartered

12 uncooked shrimp, shells on

1 lb. fresh mussels, scrubbed, rinsed, and debearded

1 cup shelled fresh or frozen peas

¼ cup freshly chopped flatleaf parsley

sea salt and freshly ground black pepper

wedges of lime or lemon, to serve

SERVES 6

Paella is the perfect dish for outdoor parties— everything can be prepared ahead of time, then you just add the ingredients in a steady stream until the whole thing comes together. But in fact, this paella is ready quite quickly so it's equally good for a midweek treat. The smell alone is wonderfully enticing, so make enough for seconds.

Heat the olive oil in a paella pan or large, deep skillet. Add the chicken thighs and chorizo and brown all over, turning frequently. Stir in the garlic, onion, and red bell pepper and cook for about 5 minutes until softened.

Stir in the rice until all the grains are coated and glossy. Add the wine and let it bubble and reduce until almost disappeared. Stir in the pepper flakes, paprika, chicken stock, and soaked saffron. Stir well, bring to a boil, and simmer gently for 10 minutes.

Stir in the tomatoes and shrimp and cook gently for 5 minutes before finally tucking the mussels into the rice and adding the peas. Cook for another 5 minutes until the mussels open (take out any that do not open after this time). At this stage, almost all the liquid will have been absorbed and the rice will be tender.

Sprinkle the chopped parsley over the top and serve immediately, straight from the pan with a big pile of lime or lemon wedges on the side. Serve with napkins.

fish pie

2 cups milk

1½ lb. finnan haddie or fresh haddock, skinned

2¾ sticks unsalted butter

1 tablespoon English mustard powder

¼ cup flour

2 hard-cooked eggs, peeled and quartered

2 lb. baking potatoes

sea salt and freshly ground black pepper

SERVES 4

If traditional fish pie conjures up memories of stodgy childhood dinners, think again! This delicious recipe is a winner on a cold evening and the mustard in the sauce provides a special flavor that you can't quite put your finger on.

Preheat the oven to 400°F.

Put the milk in a wide saucepan, heat just to boiling point, then add the fish. Turn off the heat and leave the fish to poach until opaque—do not allow it to overcook.

Meanwhile, melt 1¼ sticks of the butter in another saucepan, then stir in the mustard and flour. Remove from the heat and strain the poaching liquid into the pan.

Arrange the fish and eggs in a shallow pie dish or casserole dish.

Return the pan to the heat and, beating vigorously to smooth out any lumps, bring the mixture to a boil. Season to taste. (Take care: if you are using smoked fish, it may be salty enough.) Pour the sauce into the casserole dish and mix carefully with the fish and eggs.

Cook the potatoes in salted boiling water until soft, then drain. Return to the pan. Melt the remaining butter in a small saucepan. Reserve 4 tablespoons of this butter and stir the remainder into the potatoes. Mash well and season. Spoon the mixture carefully over the sauced fish, brush with the reserved butter, and transfer to the oven. Cook for 20 minutes, or until nicely brown.

mediterranean chunky fish stew with cheese toasts

1 small onion, finely chopped

2 garlic cloves:
1 crushed and 1 halved

a pinch of dried thyme

1 small fennel bulb (hard core removed), finely chopped

1 tablespoon olive oil

3 tablespoons dry vermouth, dry Martini, or dry white wine

2 cups tomato juice or passata

a pinch of saffron threads

freshly squeezed juice and grated peel of 1 unwaxed orange

7 oz. skinless cod fillet, cut into large chunks

4 thin slices of baguette

2 oz. Emmental or Gruyère cheese, grated

sea salt and freshly ground black pepper

SERVES 2

If you have ever tasted the classic French fish soup bouillabaisse and enjoyed the flavor, then this is a good cheat's version. The combination of saffron, orange, and fennel gives the stew its distinctive flavor. If you don't have dry vermouth on hand, use dry Martini or a dry white wine in its place. If you have time to make the base of the stew the day before you plan to eat it, the flavors will develop even further—just cook the fish at the last moment.

Heat the olive oil in a large pan, then gently sauté the onion, crushed garlic, thyme, and fennel for about 6–8 minutes or until soft. Add the dry vermouth, dry Martini, or dry white wine, and let bubble, uncovered, until the liquid has almost reduced to nothing.

Add the tomato juice or passata, saffron, orange juice and peel, and 1 cup cold water. Raise the heat and cook for 10 minutes. Add the cod and cook gently for a further 2 minutes, then season to taste.

Meanwhile, preheat the broiler to high. Toast the baguette slices on each side under the broiler until lightly golden. Rub the halved garlic over each slice and sprinkle with the grated cheese.

Ladle the stew into warmed deep serving bowls and balance the cheese-topped toasts on top. Serve immediately.

2 tablespoons vegetable oil

1 onion, grated

3 garlic cloves, crushed

2 inches fresh ginger,
peeled and sliced

1 mild red chile, chopped

1 teaspoon turmeric

2 teaspoons curry powder

1 teaspoon ground coriander

1 teaspoon ground cumin

1 lb. frozen cooked peeled shrimp,
defrosted

a 14-oz. can chopped tomatoes

freshly squeezed juice of 2 limes

a handful of cilantro, chopped

sea salt and freshly ground
black pepper

basmati rice, to serve

SERVES 4

Tiger or jumbo shrimp are ideal for this colorful, citrus-flavored curry. You really can't find a faster, easier one-bowl meal than this—or with tastier results. Serve with basmati.

shrimp curry

Heat the oil in a large pan, add the onion, garlic, ginger, and chile, and cook for 5 minutes over medium heat. Add the turmeric, curry powder, coriander, and cumin and mix well. Add the shrimp and cook for 3 minutes.

Pour in the tomatoes and lime juice, season, and bring to a boil. Reduce the heat and simmer for 5 minutes. Add the cilantro and serve with basmati rice.

easy tuna patties

20 oz. sweet potatoes,
peeled and chopped

10 oz. cooked fresh tuna or
canned tuna, flaked

2 scallions, chopped

1 egg

¾ cup cornmeal

3 tablespoons olive oil

sea salt and freshly ground
black pepper

1 lemon, to serve

tomato salad, to serve

SERVES 4

Cornmeal makes a lovely crumb coating on these patties. If using canned tuna, buy a good-quality brand that has a dense texture and large chunks. Alternatively, pan-cook fresh tuna and flake it yourself with a fork.

Cook the sweet potatoes in a pan of simmering water for 20 minutes. Drain well and mash. Add the tuna, scallions, and egg, season, and mix well. Divide the mixture into 8 equal pieces and shape into patties.

Put the cornmeal on a plate and dip the patties in it until coated on all sides.

Heat the olive oil in a skillet and fry the patties on each side until golden. Serve with lemon wedges and a tomato salad.

tuna and potato stew

1 small red bell pepper

1 small yellow bell pepper

1 small green bell pepper

3 tablespoons extra virgin olive oil

1 large onion, finely chopped

2 garlic cloves, finely chopped

5 tomatoes, peeled, seeded, and chopped (reserve any juices)

½ teaspoon sweet paprika

1 bay leaf

1 lb. potatoes, peeled and cut into ½-inch slices

2 slices of fresh tuna, 1 lb. each, cut into 6 chunky pieces each

2 tablespoons freshly torn parsley leaves

coarse sea salt and freshly ground black pepper

FRIED BREAD

6 slices of white bread, cut into triangles

extra virgin olive oil, for frying

SERVES 4–6

This is a stew from the Basque region, where fishermen used to make it on board their boats, using bonito or albacore tuna from the Bay of Biscay, and mopping up the soupy juices with lots of delicious fried bread.

Halve and seed the red, yellow, and green bell peppers and cut the flesh into ½-inch cubes.

Heat the oil in a heatproof casserole dish, add the onion, garlic, and bell peppers, and fry over low heat until softened but not colored, 12–15 minutes. Increase the heat and stir in the tomatoes and their juice. When the mixture starts to thicken, add the paprika, bay leaf, and some seasoning.

Stir in the potatoes and 1¾ cups boiling water and simmer gently for about 15 minutes until the potatoes are cooked.

Meanwhile, to make the fried bread, heat the olive oil in a large skillet, add the triangles of bread, and fry on both sides until golden. Remove and drain on paper towels.

Season the pieces of tuna 10 minutes before cooking. Add the tuna to the casserole dish and after about 30 seconds, when the underside turns pale, turn the pieces over and turn off the heat. Leave for 5 minutes. Sprinkle with parsley and serve with the triangles of fried bread.

pan-fried salmon
with cannellini bean purée

2½ oz. arugula

3½ oz. baby spinach leaves, lightly rinsed

2 oz. watercress

16 cherry tomatoes, halved

4 boneless salmon fillets, about 6½ oz. each

1 tablespoon olive oil

4 garlic cloves, halved

balsamic vinegar, for drizzling

sea salt and freshly ground black pepper

CANNELLINI BEAN PURÉE

14 oz. canned cannellini beans, drained and rinsed

1 garlic clove, crushed

1½ tablespoons freshly squeezed lemon juice

2 tablespoons freshly chopped thyme

2 teaspoons olive oil

SERVES 4

Who says you have to eat salmon with rice, potatoes, or pasta? This novel, tasty, and rather sophisticated recipe uses nutritious beans instead.

Reserve a few arugula leaves for serving then put the remaining arugula, spinach, and watercress in a salad bowl. Add the cherry tomatoes and set aside.

To make the cannellini bean purée, put the beans, garlic, lemon juice, thyme, oil, and 2 tablespoons water in a food processor or blender. Season to taste, then process to a smooth, soft purée. Add a little more water, if necessary. Transfer to a saucepan and heat gently for about 5 minutes, stirring frequently, until piping hot. Alternatively, put the purée in a microwaveable bowl, cover, and cook on HIGH for about 4 minutes, stirring halfway through, until piping hot. Let stand for 1 minute before serving.

Meanwhile, to cook the salmon fillets, heat the oil in a nonstick skillet. Add the garlic and fry gently for 1 minute. Add the salmon and cook for 5–8 minutes, turning once halfway through.

Drizzle the salad with a little balsamic vinegar, season to taste, and toss well. Put a spoonful of cannellini bean purée on each of 4 warmed serving plates. Put the reserved arugula leaves on top, followed by the salmon. Drizzle with a little extra virgin olive oil. Serve immediately with the salad.

Variation The bean purée would be delicious with most grilled foods. Try chicken, turkey, large shrimp, or tuna. Use other beans or a mixture of two or three types and keep the purée slightly chunky, if you prefer.

herb-crusted flounder and tomatoes

2 slices of seeded
whole-grain bread

grated peel and freshly squeezed
juice of ½ unwaxed lemon

1½ tablespoons freshly
grated Parmesan

2 tablespoons freshly
chopped parsley

1 tablespoon freshly
chopped thyme

1 tablespoon olive oil

four flounder fillets, or other flat
white fish fillets, such as lemon
sole, 3½ oz. each

4 ripe tomatoes, halved

sea salt and freshly ground
black pepper

SERVES 4

This quick and easy fish dinner is full of flavor. Serve with broccoli florets and small new potatoes.

Preheat the broiler to medium and lightly grease a baking sheet.

Process the bread to crumbs in a food processor, then mix in the lemon peel and juice, Parmesan, and herbs. Add the olive oil to bind the mixture together slightly, and season lightly.

Lay out the flounder fillets and tomato halves (cut-side up) on the prepared baking sheet. Press the herby crumb mixture firmly onto the fish and tomatoes. Put under the preheated broiler and cook for about 5 minutes until the crust is golden brown and the fish is cooked through. Serve immediately.

Good
add veggies

If you have a stovetop-to-oven pan, this dish can be cooked all in one pot. Use chunks of white fish such as monkfish, cod, snapper, or seabass and choose large, waxy salad potatoes, which won't break up on cooking.

fish baked with lemon, oregano, and potatoes

½ cup extra virgin olive oil

2 onions, halved and thinly sliced

2 garlic cloves, chopped

1–2 pinches of dried hot pepper flakes

1 teaspoon coriander seeds, crushed

½ teaspoon dried oregano

1½ lb. waxy potatoes, peeled and cut into wedges

2 bay leaves

5 tablespoons white wine or vermouth

½ teaspoon grated lemon peel

1½ lb. white fish (on or off the bone), cut into large chunks or steaks

2 small lemons, halved

1 tablespoon freshly chopped oregano

1 tablespoon freshly chopped flatleaf parsley

sea salt and freshly ground black pepper

SERVES 4

Preheat the oven to 400°F.

Heat a large skillet or ovenproof lidded skillet over medium heat and add the oil. Add the onion and fry for 2–3 minutes, then turn the heat right down. Add 1–2 pinches of salt, cover, and let the onion cook very gently for 10–12 minutes until soft and golden yellow. Add the garlic, pepper flakes, crushed coriander seeds, and dried oregano. Cook for another 3–4 minutes.

Add the potatoes and bay leaves to the skillet, turning them in the oily onions. Season generously. Cook for a few minutes, then add the wine and lemon peel. When it bubbles, cover and cook gently for 15–20 minutes or until the potatoes are just tender.

Transfer the potatoes to a large ovenproof baking dish, if necessary. Season the fish with a little salt, then nestle into the potatoes. Squeeze a little lemon juice from one of the lemon halves over the fish and spoon over a little of the oily juices. Add the lemon halves to the dish and turn in the oil.

Bake, uncovered, in the preheated oven for 20–25 minutes, basting once or twice, until the potatoes are tender and the fish cooked through. Serve sprinkled with fresh oregano and parsley.

DESSERTS & SWEET TREATS

You can't go wrong with crumble, and this simple plum crumble is a great favorite with children, especially when made with Victoria plums. Plums have such a rich flavor when they are cooked that they need little or no other flavorings. Experiment with greengages, Santa Rosas, or Queen Anne plums.

simple plum crumble

8–10 ripe plums

4–5 tablespoons sugar

light cream, to serve

CRUMBLE TOPPING

1⅓ cups all-purpose flour

½ stick plus 1 tablespoon unsalted butter, chilled

a pinch of salt

¼ cup superfine sugar

a medium, shallow, ovenproof dish

SERVES 4–6

Preheat the oven to 350°F and set a baking sheet on the middle shelf to heat.

Halve the plums and remove the pits. Cut the halves into quarters if they are very large. Toss them with the sugar and tip them into the ovenproof dish.

To make the topping, put the flour, butter, and salt in a bowl and rub together with your fingertips until the mixture resembles bread crumbs. Stir in the sugar. (At this point the mixture can be popped in a plastic bag and chilled until ready to cook.)

Lightly scatter the topping mixture over the plums. Place the dish on the baking sheet in the preheated oven and bake for 40–45 minutes, until golden brown. Serve with light cream.

almond fruit crumble

20 oz. fruit

¼ cup packed brown sugar

custard sauce, cream, or ice cream,
to serve

CRUMBLE TOPPING

1 cup self-rising flour

1 teaspoon baking powder

1 stick unsalted butter, diced

¼ cup natural cane sugar

⅓ cup ground almonds

⅓ cup old-fashioned rolled oats

a 1-quart ovenproof dish, greased

SERVES 4

Any combination of fruits would sit well under this toasty, crunchy, almondy crumble. Try rhubarb and ginger, apple and apricot, pear and blackcurrant, or whatever's in the fruit bowl.

Preheat the oven to 375°F.

Put the fruit in the prepared ovenproof dish and add the brown sugar and ⅓ cup water.

To make the topping, put the flour, baking powder, and butter in a bowl and rub together with your fingertips until the mixture resembles coarse bread crumbs. Stir in the cane sugar, almonds, and oats.

Lightly scatter the topping mixture over the fruit. Bake in the preheated oven for 30 minutes. The crumble should be golden and the fruit bubbling up around the edges. Serve with custard sauce, cream, or ice cream.

buttered apricot betty

1½ lb. fresh apricots or
three 14-oz. cans apricots
in natural juice

3 cups fresh bread crumbs,
lightly toasted

1 stick unsalted butter, diced

2 tablespoons corn or
golden syrup

½ cup freshly squeezed
orange juice

¼ cup superfine sugar

cream, to serve

*a medium, ovenproof,
deep pie dish, greased*

a large roasting pan

SERVES 4

If you have the patience, you can crack the apricot pits and take out the kernels inside. These are very like bitter almonds, and are a fantastic addition when chopped and toasted with the bread crumbs.

Preheat the oven to 375°F.

Halve the fresh apricots and flip out the pits, or drain the canned apricots and pat dry. Place a layer of apricots in the prepared pie dish.

Reserve 4–6 tablespoons of the bread crumbs for the top. Sprinkle some of the rest of the bread crumbs over the apricots, and dot with some of the butter. Put in some more apricots and repeat these alternate casual layers until all the apricots and bread crumbs are used up. Use the reserved bread crumbs for the final top layer.

Warm the syrup with the orange juice, and pour this over the top. Sprinkle with sugar and dot with the remaining butter.

Place the pie dish in the roasting pan and pour in enough boiling water to come halfway up the sides of the dish. (This is a *bain-marie*.) Bake in the preheated oven for 45 minutes, or until the apricots are soft and the top crispy and brown. Serve warm, not hot, with cream.

This is a gorgeously moist, tangy treat to satisfy a sweet tooth after a light meal, and it is special enough to serve when you have guests, too. Cornmeal is a useful ingredient which gives cakes a slightly coarser, crunchier texture than wheat flour.

lemon cornmeal cake

1½ sticks unsalted butter, softened

¾ cup natural cane sugar

¾ cup cornmeal

½ teaspoon baking powder

1 cup ground almonds

grated peel and freshly squeezed juice of 1 unwaxed lemon

½ teaspoon pure vanilla extract

3 eggs

plain yogurt, to serve

SYRUP

grated peel and freshly squeezed juice of 2 unwaxed lemons

¼ cup natural cane sugar

a springform cake pan, 10 inches in diameter, lightly greased

SERVES 6–8

Preheat the oven to 350°F.

Beat together the butter and sugar until creamy. Add the cornmeal, baking powder, ground almonds, lemon peel and juice, vanilla extract, and eggs. Mix together until smooth.

Spoon the mixture into the prepared pan and bake in the middle of the preheated oven for 30 minutes.

Meanwhile, make the syrup. Put the lemon peel and juice in a small saucepan with the sugar and 2 tablespoons water. Bring to a boil and simmer for 2 minutes. When the cake is done, let cool slightly in the pan, then turn out and pierce all over with a fine skewer. Spoon the syrup over the cake, then set aside for 20 minutes while it is absorbed. Serve with plain yogurt.

It's easy to think your brownies aren't cooked and to give them those extra few minutes, which can dry them out and turn them into a mealy chocolate cake. So be brave: if the mixture doesn't wobble in the middle and a skewer inserted in the center comes out chocolatey, remove the brownies from the oven and by the time they have cooled, they will be perfect.

chocolate brownies with
vanilla-flecked crème fraîche

8 oz. semisweet chocolate, broken into pieces, plus extra to serve

2 sticks unsalted butter, softened

4 large eggs, beaten

1²⁄₃ cups sugar

½ teaspoon fine salt

1 cup self-rising flour

2 tablespoons unsweetened cocoa powder

¾ cup crème fraîche or very lightly whipped heavy cream

1 vanilla bean, cut lengthwise

a baking pan, 8 x 12 inches, greased and lined with parchment paper

MAKES 16

Preheat the oven to 350°F. Don't use a convection oven if you have the choice, as it dries the outside of the brownies.

Put the chocolate and butter in a heatproof bowl set over a pan of simmering water and leave for several minutes until melted, then remove from the pan and let cool.

Beat together the eggs and the sugar with an electric mixer. Pour in the cooled chocolate mixture, then add the salt and finally the flour. Beat until well blended. Pour the mixture into the prepared baking pan and bake in the center of the preheated oven for 23–25 minutes (you have to be precise with brownies!). The outside should look crackled and the inside feel firm to the touch but will be gooey underneath. Remove from the oven and let cool in the pan for 15 minutes, then slice into squares.

Mix the crème fraîche or cream with the vanilla seeds scraped from the bean and serve with a brownie square or two. Grate some extra chocolate over the top.

This really is comfort food at its most tempting. This French version uses the double rice-cooking method—blanching the rice first removes much of the starch. The result is light and delicate, not blobby and glutinous like some puddings. Serve it with red fruit coulis, or chocolate, cranberry, or custard sauce. Of course, it's also very nice just as it is.

rice pudding

½ cup risotto rice, such as arborio

2 cups whole milk, boiled

⅓ cup sugar

1 vanilla bean, cut lengthwise

1 tablespoon unsalted butter

a pinch of salt

SERVES 4

Preheat the oven to 350°F.

Put the rice in a saucepan and add cold water to cover. Slowly bring to a boil over medium heat, then boil for 5 minutes. Drain the rice and rinse under cold water. Set aside to drain well.

Meanwhile, put the milk in an ovenproof pan with a lid and bring to a boil. Add the sugar and vanilla bean. Remove from the heat, cover, and set aside for 15 minutes. Scrape the vanilla seeds from the bean and stir them through the milk.

Add the rice to the milk, then add the butter and salt. Bring slowly to a boil. Cover and transfer to the preheated oven. Do not stir. Cook until the rice is tender and the liquid is almost completely absorbed but not dry, about 25–35 minutes. Serve warm.

The tartness and spiciness of the apples here cuts through the sweet, buttery toffee sauce. Sticky toffee sauce is very versatile and can be served with ice cream or spooned over other baked fruit, such as bananas, pears, peaches, or apricots. The apples can be prepared in the morning and popped into the oven as soon as you get home.

cream or vanilla ice cream,
to serve

STICKY TOFFEE SAUCE

5 tablespoons unsalted butter

⅓ cup packed brown sugar

5 tablespoons heavy cream

STUFFED APPLES

⅓ cup dried dates, roughly chopped

½ oz. stem ginger in syrup,
drained and finely chopped

2 tablespoons walnuts or pecan
nuts, roughly chopped

4 large cooking apples, such as
Granny Smith or Courtland, cored

SERVES 4

baked apples with dates and sticky toffee sauce

Preheat the oven to 300°F.

First make the sticky toffee sauce. Put the butter, sugar, and cream in a pan over low heat until melted. Bring to a boil and cook for 1 minute. Remove from the heat and set aside.

To make the stuffed apples, mix together the dates, ginger, and walnuts or pecan nuts. Stuff half this mixture into the cored apples and stir the remainder into the toffee sauce.

Arrange the stuffed apples in an ovenproof dish or roasting pan so that they fit tightly. Pour the toffee sauce over the apples and cover the entire dish or pan with aluminum foil.

Bake in the preheated oven for 25–30 minutes, basting the apples with the sauce occasionally. Remove the dish or pan from the oven and let the apples cool for 2 minutes. Serve while still warm, with cream or vanilla ice cream.

bread and butter puddings

1¼ cups milk

1¼ cups heavy cream

½ teaspoon pure vanilla extract

¼ cup sugar

3 eggs

6 thick slices of brioche bread or hot cross buns, halved

⅓ cup golden raisins

freshly grated nutmeg, to sprinkle

6 ramekins, 1 cup each, well greased

SERVES 6

This is unbeatable comfort food. Made with brioche or hot cross buns for extra flavor, these individual puddings cook in under 20 minutes.

Preheat the oven to 350°F.

Put the milk, cream, vanilla extract, and 3 tablespoons of the sugar into a saucepan and heat until the sugar dissolves.

Put the eggs into a bowl and beat well. Stir in 2–3 tablespoons of the hot milk mixture to warm the eggs, then stir in the remainder of the hot milk. You should have a custard-like mixture.

Lightly toast the brioche or hot cross buns and cut into quarters. Divide between the prepared ramekins and sprinkle with the raisins.

Pour in the custard, grate a little nutmeg over the top, then sprinkle with the remaining sugar. Bake in the preheated oven for 18–20 minutes until firm. Let cool a little, then serve warm.

This is a very simple recipe, a bit like a frangipane and fruit tart, but without the fuss of dough making. They must be eaten soon after baking, but the almond filling can be made several hours in advance and refrigerated until needed, and you can hollow out the peaches at the same time. If you don't have a muffin pan, make little rings out of foil to keep the peaches upright while baking.

3 tablespoons unsalted butter, at room temperature

3 tablespoons sugar

1 large egg

½ cup ground almonds

1 oz. finely crushed amaretti cookies

6 ripe peaches

thick plain yogurt or sour cream, to serve

RASPBERRY SAUCE

1 cup fresh raspberries (or frozen and thawed)

1 tablespoon confectioners' sugar

1 tablespoon freshly squeezed lemon juice

a 12-cup muffin pan

SERVES 6

baked amaretti peaches
with raspberry sauce

Preheat the oven to 350°F.

Put the butter and sugar in a bowl and beat until blended. Beat in the egg. Stir in the ground almonds and amaretti until well mixed. Set aside.

Cut the peaches in half and remove the pits. Using a small spoon, scrape out a bit more from each hollow to make more space for the filling (not too much). Divide the filling between the peaches, spooning some into each hollow. Put a peach half into each muffin cup to keep them upright while baking.

Bake in the preheated oven until the filling is puffed and golden, about 25–30 minutes.

Meanwhile, to make the sauce, put the raspberries, confectioners' sugar, and lemon juice in a small food processor and purée. Set aside.

Serve the peaches warm with the raspberry sauce.

double chocolate muffins

1¾ cups all-purpose flour

½ cup unsweetened cocoa powder

2 teaspoons baking powder

½ cup sugar

½ cup semisweet chocolate chips, plus extra to sprinkle

2 extra-large eggs

1 cup milk

½ cup safflower oil

1 teaspoon pure vanilla extract

a 12-cup muffin pan, lined with paper liners

MAKES 12

Everybody loves chocolate muffins! These are quick to prepare and made with cocoa powder plus chocolate chips for maximum chocolate flavor.

Preheat the oven to 400°F.

Set a large fine-mesh sieve over a large bowl. Tip the flour, cocoa, baking powder, and sugar into the sieve and sift into the bowl. Add the chocolate chips.

Break the eggs into a second bowl. Add the milk, oil, and vanilla extract, then mix well with a fork. Add the flour mixture and gently stir with a wooden spoon.

Spoon the mixture into the paper liners—each one should be about half full. Sprinkle with extra chocolate chips.

Bake in the preheated oven for about 20 minutes until well-risen and just firm. Remove from the oven and turn the muffins out onto a wire rack to cool for about 30 minutes. These muffins are best eaten the same day.

This delightfully fresh-tasting pudding is based on a traditional British recipe. Served warm (it's best that way), the bottom layer forms a tangy, lemony sauce for the light sponge layer, but it is also delicious cold (see Variation), when the sauce sets into a light custard that is lovely with the taste of blackberries. So there you are—two recipes for the price of one!

lemon and blackberry puddings

6–8 oz. ripe blackberries

½ cup sugar, plus 1 tablespoon

½ stick butter, softened

1 vanilla bean, cut lengthwise

grated peel and freshly squeezed juice of 1 large unwaxed lemon

2 large eggs, separated

2 slightly heaping tablespoons all-purpose flour

1 cup milk

4 tablespoons whipping cream, plus extra to serve (optional)

½ teaspoon cream of tartar

4–5 small ovenproof dishes, greased

SERVES 4–5

Preheat the oven to 350°F.

Put the blackberries and the 1 tablespoon sugar in a bowl, toss gently, then spoon into the dishes.

Put the butter and the remaining sugar in a bowl and beat until creamy. Scrape the seeds from the vanilla bean into the mixture and beat to mix. Beat in the lemon peel, followed by the egg yolks. Sift in the flour, stir in, then gradually beat in the milk, cream, and lemon juice.

Put the egg whites and cream of tartar in a separate, grease-free bowl and beat until stiff but not dry. Beat 2 tablespoons of the egg whites into the pudding mixture, then fold in the remainder with a spatula. Spoon the mixture into the prepared dishes and bake in the preheated oven for 30–35 minutes. Serve hot or warm, with cream, if you like.

Variation To serve cold, bake in a 1-quart shallow ovenproof dish for an additional 5–10 minutes. Let cool, then chill. Beat 1 scant cup whipping cream and 2 tablespoons vanilla sugar in a bowl until thick. Spread over the pudding and decorate with blackberries and lemon peel.

yogurt cake

a pot of plain set yogurt

2 pots of sugar

3 pots of flour

2 eggs

1 tablespoon safflower oil

1 teaspoon baking soda

a pinch of salt

freshly squeezed juice of 1 orange

1 tablespoon confectioners' sugar, to decorate

a deep cake pan, 9 inches in diameter, greased

SERVES 8

This is such a simple cake that there's no excuse not to serve it up for dessert. The yogurt pot is the measure, so it doesn't really matter what size you use. If you don't fancy orange, try other flavorings: cinnamon, honey, vanilla, chocolate, fruit pieces, etc. This is great to make, and eat, with children.

Preheat the oven to 350°F.

Empty the yogurt into a large bowl and wipe out the pot so when you measure the other ingredients, they won't stick. Add the sugar, flour, eggs, oil, baking soda, salt, and half the orange juice. Stir well.

Pour into the prepared cake pan and bake in the preheated oven until a knife inserted in the middle comes out clean, about 15–20 minutes. Remove from the oven and pierce a few holes in the top with a fork. Pour over the remaining orange juice. Let cool slightly, then turn out onto a wire rack to cool. Dust with confectioners' sugar and serve at room temperature.

Sweet, sticky, and indulgent, these little plum fudge desserts can be prepared in advance, then cooked just before serving. Making them in individual ramekins means they look special enough to serve up at a dinner party, too.

½ stick unsalted butter

4–5 tablespoons honey

2 tablespoons heavy cream

2 tablespoons brown sugar

1 teaspoon apple pie spice

1½ cups fresh white bread crumbs

2 ripe plums, halved, pitted, and thinly sliced

sour cream, to serve

4 ramekins, ⅔ cup each

SERVES 4

plum fudge desserts

Preheat the oven to 400°F.

Put the butter, honey, and cream in a saucepan and heat until melted. Put the sugar, apple pie spice, and bread crumbs in a bowl and stir well.

Divide half the buttery fudge mixture between the ramekins and top with a layer of plum slices and half the bread-crumb mix. Add the remaining plums and bread crumbs, then spoon over the remaining sauce.

Put the ramekins on a baking sheet and bake in the preheated oven for 20 minutes. Remove from the oven and let cool for 5 minutes, then carefully unmold the puddings and serve with a spoonful of sour cream.

raspberry and ginger tiramisu

²/₃ cup raspberries

2 teaspoons sugar

8 ladyfingers (savoiardi biscuits)

½ cup cooled, strong black coffee, such as espresso

⅓ cup coffee-flavor liqueur, such as Tia Maria or Kahlúa, or a cream liqueur, such as Baileys

8 oz. mascarpone cheese

¼ cup confectioners' sugar

1 teaspoon ground ginger

1 tablespoon milk

unsweetened cocoa powder, for dusting

a few pinches of ground cinnamon

4 glass sundae dishes, Martini glasses, or large wine glasses

SERVES 4

This quick and easy recipe is a winner when you've got friends coming over for dinner straight after work, as it can be assembled in the morning and left in the fridge to improve during the day. It's useful to always keep a packet of ladyfingers in the pantry and a tub of mascarpone in the fridge for occasions such as these. A strong black freshly made espresso will give you a more intense and authentic flavor, but you can use an instant coffee (made fairly strong), if preferred.

Put the raspberries in a bowl, add the sugar, and lightly mash with a fork. Spoon the fruit into the sundae dishes, Martini glasses, or large wine glasses.

Pour the coffee and liqueur into a small bowl and mix together. Dip both ends of the ladyfingers in the coffee mixture so that they absorb the liquid and darken in color, then put them on top of the raspberries. Use your fingers to press the ladyfingers down a little to fit the glass.

Put the mascarpone, confectioners' sugar, and ginger in a large bowl and beat to combine. Gradually beat in the milk to form a smooth, creamy mixture. Spoon this mixture over the ladyfingers. Dust with a little cocoa powder and sprinkle a pinch of cinnamon over each glass.

Serve immediately or refrigerate until ready to serve.

Variation You could use amaretti instead of the ladyfingers. They give the dessert a lovely almond flavor.

This is a wonderful way of cooking pears. It is so simple to make, but tastes very luxurious. Choose pears that are ripe but not too soft, or they will overcook in the oven. If you can't get a good rich Marsala or Vin Santo, use sweet sherry or Madeira instead.

caramelized pears with
marsala and mascarpone cream

6 large ripe pears

¾ cup sugar

⅔ cup Marsala or Vin Santo

8 oz. mascarpone cheese

1 vanilla bean, cut lengthwise

a flameproof, ovenproof pan or dish

SERVES 6

Preheat the oven to 375°F.

Cut the pears in half and scoop out the cores—do not peel them. Sprinkle the sugar into the pan or dish. Set over medium heat and let the sugar melt and caramelize. Remove from the heat as soon as it reaches a medium-brown color and quickly arrange the pears cut-side down in the caramel.

Bake in the preheated oven until the pears are soft, 20–25 minutes. Carefully lift out the pears and transfer to an ovenproof serving dish, keeping the caramel in the pan.

Put the pan on top of the stove over medium heat and add the Marsala or Vin Santo. Bring to a boil, stirring to dislodge any set caramel, and boil fast until reduced and syrupy. Set aside.

Scoop out a good teaspoon from each cooked pear and put it in a bowl. Add the mascarpone and the seeds scraped from the vanilla bean and beat well. Fill the centers of the pears with the mascarpone mixture. Return to the oven for 5 minutes until it has heated through. Serve with the caramel sauce spooned over the top.

cheat's cherry brûlée

1¼ lb. ripe cherries, pitted

⅓ cup light cream

⅓ cup reduced-fat cream cheese

1 teaspoon pure vanilla extract

¼ cup brown sugar

4 ramekins, ¾ cup each

SERVES 4

A slightly healthier and much quicker version of the traditional crème brûlée, this can be made with fresh, ripe cherries or plums.

Preheat the broiler to hot.

Put the cherries in a saucepan with ½ cup water. Cook over high heat until simmering, then lower the heat and simmer gently until the cherries have slightly softened, 5–7 minutes. Remove the pan from the heat.

Put the light cream, cream cheese, and vanilla extract in a bowl and mix well. Divide the cherries between the ramekins. Spoon the cream mixture over the fruit, then top with 1 tablespoon of the brown sugar.

Put the ramekins under the preheated broiler until the sugar melts and begins to caramelize. Remove from the heat and serve.

Variation If you are making this dessert for a special occasion, soak the cherries in 2–3 tablespoons kirsch liqueur or cherry brandy before topping with the cream mixture. If you prefer a cold dessert, put the brûlées in the fridge to chill. This will make the sugar set, making it even crunchier.

Ready-made phyllo pastry works well here, and it doesn't matter what it looks like when it goes into the oven. When it's baked and dusted with confectioners' sugar, your strudel will taste and look sensational. Choose slightly tart, well-flavored apples.

apple strudel

1½ oz. amaretti cookies

8 oz. phyllo pastry dough

4 tablespoons unsalted butter, melted

4 medium apples (1¾ lb.), peeled, cored, and sliced

a generous ⅓ cup sugar

1½ teaspoons ground cinnamon

2 tablespoons raisins, slivered almonds, or dried blueberries

confectioners' sugar, for dusting

ice cream or yogurt, to serve

a large baking sheet, greased

SERVES 6

Preheat the oven to 400°F.

Put the amaretti cookies in a plastic bag and crush with a rolling pin.

Arrange the phyllo dough in overlapping sheets to make a rectangle about 22 x 28 inches. You should have several layers of dough overlapping. Using a pastry brush, lightly brush about half the melted butter over the dough. Sprinkle the amaretti crumbs on top, then add the apple slices, leaving a clear border of about 2 inches all around the edges. Sprinkle with the sugar and cinnamon, then add the raisins, almonds, or blueberries.

To roll up the strudel, first fold over the dough borders along the two short sides, then fold over the dough border along one long side. Roll up the strudel from this side, and don't worry if the dough splits and the filling falls out, just push it all back together with your hands. Transfer the strudel to the prepared baking sheet with the help of a couple of spatulas, if necessary. If the strudel is too big for the baking sheet you may have to curve it into a horseshoe. Brush all over with the rest of the melted butter.

Bake in the preheated oven for 35 minutes, or until golden brown. Remove from the oven and dust with confectioners' sugar. Cut into thick slices and eat warm or at room temperature with ice cream or yogurt.

A family favorite in French homes, this is the dessert to make for anyone who likes custard and sweet summer berries. The optional drizzle of rum at the end is strictly for the adults. You can also use ground almonds instead of the flour.

cherry clafoutis

2 cups milk

1 vanilla bean, cut lengthwise

3 eggs

a pinch of salt

5 tablespoons superfine sugar, plus extra for dredging

¼ cup all-purpose flour

1½ lb. fresh or frozen cherries

½ stick unsalted butter, chilled and diced

a little dark rum (optional)

a medium, shallow baking dish

SERVES 4

Preheat the oven to 425°F.

Heat the milk and seeds scraped from the vanilla bean to blood temperature—you should be able to hold a finger in the liquid and count to ten without any pain.

Beat the eggs lightly with the salt and sugar until pale, then beat in the flour. Pour in the warmed milk, stirring to mix. Scatter the cherries in the baking dish and pour the batter over them. Dot with pieces of butter and bake in the preheated oven for about 25–30 minutes or until the batter is puffed up and set around the cherries.

Remove from the oven and sprinkle with rum, if using, and liberally dredge with sugar before serving warm.

Everybody loves pavlova—adults and children alike. Raspberries are delicious with hazelnut and chocolate, but cherries and strawberries would also work well. Keep the cooled meringue in an airtight box until ready to use. You can make this up to one day ahead.

hazelnut and raspberry pavlova with hot chocolate sauce

4 extra-large egg whites

a pinch of sea salt

1¼ cups sugar, plus a little extra, to taste

1 teaspoon cornstarch

1 teaspoon pure vanilla extract

1 teaspoon wine vinegar

⅔ cup toasted chopped hazelnuts, plus extra for sprinkling

8 oz. raspberries

HOT CHOCOLATE SAUCE AND WHIPPED CREAM

7 oz. bittersweet chocolate, chopped

2¾ cups heavy cream

¼ cup sugar, plus 1 tablespoon extra

2 tablespoons unsalted butter

a baking sheet, lined with nonstick parchment paper

SERVES 6

Preheat the oven to 275°F. Mark the parchment paper on the baking sheet with a 10-inch circle.

Put the egg whites and salt in a bowl and beat until very stiff. Gradually beat in the sugar, a large spoonful at a time, making sure the meringue is "bouncily" stiff before adding the next spoonful. Beat the cornstarch, vanilla extract, and vinegar into the meringue. Fold in the hazelnuts.

Spoon the meringue into the circle on the baking sheet right to the edges, making it as rough as you like, but not too shallow. Make a slight dip in the center.

Bake in the preheated oven for about 45 minutes until just beginning to turn the palest brown. Turn off the oven and let cool slowly in the oven.

To make the hot chocolate sauce, put the chocolate, 1 cup of the cream, the sugar, and butter in a saucepan. Stir until melted. Pour into a pitcher and keep it warm. Put the 1 tablespoon sugar and remaining cream in a bowl and whip until soft peaks form.

Carefully peel the parchment paper from the pavlova and set it on a serving dish. Dollop the cream generously on top and sprinkle with the raspberries. Trail the hot chocolate sauce over the top. Serve immediately.

Chocolate, butter, eggs, and sugar; who needs flour? This is child's play to make and is best when made in advance—ideal for entertaining. It's supposed to be crumbly and almost raw in the middle, so if you're nervous about baking in public, this is the dessert for you because it always looks good. It is also the perfect after-dinner cake, rich and satisfying, and a nice companion when lingering over coffee after dinner.

flourless chocolate cake

7 oz. best-quality bittersweet chocolate, broken into pieces

1½ sticks unsalted butter, cubed

5 extra-large eggs, separated

⅔ cup sugar

raspberries, to serve (optional)

cream, to serve (optional)

a nonstick springform cake pan, 9 inches in diameter

SERVES 6–8

Preheat the oven to 350°F.

Put the chocolate and butter in a heatproof bowl set over a pan of simmering water and leave for several minutes until melted, then remove from the pan and let cool slightly.

Put the egg yolks and all but 2 tablespoons of the sugar in a large bowl. Beat vigorously until pale and fluffy, about 5 minutes. Set aside.

Put the egg whites in another bowl and beat on high until firm. Add the remaining 2 tablespoons sugar and continue beating until stiff peaks form. Set aside.

Stir the chocolate mixture into the egg yolk mixture and blend well. Add a third of the beaten whites and mix well until there are no white streaks. Carefully fold in the remaining whites, using a rubber spatula, until there are no white streaks. Pour into the cake pan and set it on a baking sheet.

Bake in the preheated oven until crisp around the edges, but still jiggly and almost raw looking in the very middle, 20–30 minutes. Let cool slightly, then run a knife around the inside edge of the pan to loosen and remove the outer ring. Serve at room temperature with raspberries and cream, if you like.

fruity carrot cake

6 tablespoons sunflower oil

½ cup unrefined light brown sugar

1 egg, beaten

3 egg whites

6 oz. carrots,
peeled and coarsely grated

1 cooking apple, peeled, cored,
and grated

1¼ cups golden raisins

½ cup prunes, chopped

¼ cup dried apricots, chopped

⅓ cup dried blueberries or
sour cherries

1 teaspoon ground cinnamon

1 teaspoon baking powder

2¼ cups stoneground
whole-wheat flour

⅓ cup self-rising flour

2 teaspoons brown sugar

*a deep cake pan, 8 inches in diameter,
greased and lined with
parchment paper*

MAKES 12 SLICES

This delicious, moist cake is packed full of fruits—from prunes and dried apricots to grated fresh apple. Treat yourself to a slice with a midafternoon cup of tea, or pop a little portion in the children's lunchboxes.

Preheat the oven to 325°F.

Pour the oil into a large bowl, add the sugar, and beat until smooth and free from lumps. Beat in the whole egg and the egg whites, a little at a time. Add the carrot, apple, and dried fruit and stir well.

Sift the cinnamon, baking powder, and flours into the mixture, adding any bran left in the strainer to the bowl. Stir gently until incorporated. Do not overmix. Spoon the mixture into the prepared cake pan. Level the top with a spatula or round-bladed knife, then sprinkle the top with the brown sugar.

Bake in the preheated oven for 1¼ hours, or until a skewer inserted into the center comes out clean. Remove from the oven and let cool in the pan before turning out. Store in an airtight container for up to 1 week.

A classic Victoria sponge cake filled with cream and fresh fruit makes a wonderful centerpiece for a traditional afternoon tea. Make it in the summer when strawberries are in season and at their juicy and fragrant best.

victoria sponge cake
with strawberries and cream

6 oz. unsalted butter, at room temperature

¾ cup plus 2 tablespoons sugar

3 eggs

1½ cups self-rising flour

3½ tablespoons good-quality strawberry jam

1 cup strawberries, hulled and halved or quartered, depending on size

½ cup whipping cream

confectioners' sugar, for dusting

two 8-inch cake pans with removable bottoms, greased and baselined with parchment paper

SERVES 6–8

Preheat the oven to 350°F.

Beat together the butter and sugar in a large bowl until pale and fluffy. Beat in the eggs one at a time. Sift the flour into the mixture and fold in until thoroughly combined.

Spoon the cake mixture into the prepared pans and spread out evenly using the back of the spoon. Bake in the preheated oven for 20–25 minutes until golden brown and the sponge springs back when pressed gently with the tips of your fingers. Turn out the cakes onto a wire rack, gently peel off the parchment paper, and let cool completely.

Slice a thin sliver off the top of one of the cakes to create a flat surface. Spread the strawberry jam over the surface and top with the strawberries. Whip the cream until it stands in soft peaks, then spread on top of the strawberries. Top with the second cake, press down gently, and dust with confectioners' sugar.

oat and chocolate cookies

2 sticks butter, softened

¼ cup sugar

½ cup packed light brown sugar

4 oz. semisweet chocolate chips

1¾ cups old-fashioned rolled oats

1½ cups self-rising flour

MAKES 15–20

These much-loved cookies will go down a treat with hungry children when they come home from school.

Preheat the oven to 350°F.

Beat the butter and sugars together until pale and creamy. Stir in the chocolate chips and oats. Add the flour and mix well.

Using your hands, form the mixture into 15–20 small balls. Flatten slightly with your palms and place them on a baking sheet, allowing room for growth. Bake in the preheated oven for 15–20 minutes. Transfer to a wire rack to cool, then store in an airtight container.

pumpkin seed cookies

1½ cups self-rising flour

1 stick butter, diced

⅔ cup packed light brown sugar

1 egg, beaten

½ cup pumpkin seeds

MAKES 20

Seeds contain lots of nutrients that are an important part of a good diet. A great way to feed them to your family is to hide them in these tasty cookies.

Preheat the oven to 350°F.

Put the flour, butter, and sugar in a bowl and mix with a fork until the mixture resembles bread crumbs. Add the egg and seeds, mix again, and form into a ball.

Lightly flour a work surface and use your hands to roll the dough into a sausage shape about 8 inches long. Cut into 20 slices and place on a nonstick or greased baking sheet. Bake in the preheated oven for 12–15 minutes. Transfer to a wire rack to cool, then store in an airtight container.

Kids will love to help you make these gingerbread people. Look out for cookie cutters (in specialist kitchen stores) in the shape of a princess, teddy bear, Santa, or any other favorite character.

gingerbread people

2½ cups self-rising flour

a pinch of salt

1 tablespoon ground ginger

1 cup sugar

1 stick unsalted butter

¼ cup light corn syrup

1 extra-large egg, beaten

TO DECORATE

raisins

edible silver balls

colored chocolate buttons

2 or more baking sheets, greased

shaped cookie cutters

MAKES ABOUT 14 FIGURES

Preheat the oven to 325°F.

Sift the flour, salt, and ground ginger into a large bowl. Add the sugar and mix in with a wooden spoon. Make a hollow in the center.

Put the butter and syrup in a small saucepan. Heat very gently until melted—don't let the mixture become hot. Carefully pour into the hollow in the flour mixture. Pour the egg into the hollow on top of the melted mixture. Mix all the ingredients with a wooden spoon. As soon as the dough starts to come together, push it together into a ball. If it is too hot to handle, wait for it to cool.

Turn the dough out onto a work surface lightly dusted with flour. Gently roll out the dough to a large rectangle about ¼ inch thick. Cut out figures with the cookie cutters, then transfer them to the prepared baking sheets, allowing room for growth. Gather the trimmings into a ball, then roll out and cut more figures as before.

Decorate the figures with raisins, silver balls, or chocolate buttons. Bake in the preheated oven for about 15 minutes until golden brown. Watch them carefully, because they can quickly burn.

Remove from the oven and let cool on the sheets for 5 minutes. When the figures are firm, transfer to a wire rack. Cool completely and store in an airtight container for up to 1 week.

nutty chocolate and marshmallow on toast

2 thick slices of white bread

2 tablespoons light cream

½ oz. semisweet chocolate, grated or shaved, or good-quality chocolate chips

a handful of pecan nuts

a handful of mini-marshmallows

SERVES 2

Sinfully sweet and sticky, this toast is the ultimate in instant comfort food. It's lacking sophistication by anyone's standards, but it makes a luscious treat when you're feeling blue and need a no-effort pick-me-up.

Preheat the broiler to medium.

Toast the bread on one side under the preheated broiler, then flip over. Pour the cream over the untoasted side, sprinkle with the grated or shaved chocolate, nuts, and marshmallows and broil until golden and bubbling. Eat with caution: the topping will be very hot!

Note This is definitely a recipe for those with a sweet tooth. You can use any type of white bread—a classic square white loaf, a French country loaf, or several slices of white baguette cut on the diagonal. However, don't be tempted to try it with a sweet bread such as brioche or panettone—there's only so much sugar you should eat at once!

DRINKS

chilled lemon grass tisane

1–2 red chiles, seeded and sliced

2–4 lemon grass stalks, outer leaves discarded, inner section finely sliced

2 inches fresh ginger, peeled and sliced

¼ cup sugar

freshly squeezed juice of 2 lemons

mint leaves and ice cubes, to serve

SERVES 4

Tisane is the French word for an infusion of herbs, flowers, or other aromatics. This is an unusual, deliciously spicy version, which is chilled down to make a great contrast between hot and cold.

Put the chile into a heatproof bowl with the lemon grass, ginger, and sugar, then add 1 quart boiling water and the lemon juice and stir to dissolve the sugar. Let infuse until cold.

Strain the cooled liquid and chill for at least 30 minutes. Serve in tall glasses with mint leaves and ice cubes.

orange and apple refresher

2 large oranges, peeled

2 Granny Smith apples

1 inch fresh ginger, peeled

ice cubes, to serve

a juicing machine

SERVES 2

This is the kind of zingy pick-me-up you need first thing in the morning to get you off to a great start.

Push the oranges, apples, and ginger through the juicer. Half-fill 2 tall glasses with ice cubes, pour the juice over the top, and serve.

This utterly delicious juice combo is a super-healthy way to start the day—kiwi fruit contains large amounts of vitamin C. If you're feeling brave, add a little watercress or arugula for a green, peppery hit. Juices and smoothies taste much better if the fruit is only just ripe (or even a little underripe); if too ripe, the taste will be dull. Transform this into a yogurt smoothie in a blender, in which case it will serve two.

pear, apple, and kiwi fruit juice with ginger

1 not-too-ripe pear

1 apple

2 not-too-ripe kiwi fruit

1 inch fresh ginger, peeled and coarsely chopped

SERVES 1

Juicer method Peel and core the pear and apple and cut into 6 wedges each. Peel and quarter the kiwi fruit. Put the pear through the juicer first, followed by the ginger, kiwi fruit, and finally the apple. Stir well before serving, because it can separate. Drink as soon as possible and just feel those vitamins coursing through your body!

Blender smoothie Put all the prepared fruits and ginger in a blender with ⅔ cup plain yogurt. Blend until smooth, adding a squeeze of lemon juice or a little salt to taste.

passion fruit and papaya blitz

1 orange

3 ice cubes

1 ripe papaya

2 passion fruit, halved

SERVES 1

A refreshing taste of the exotic for any time of day, but especially good on a hot summer's afternoon.

Squeeze the juice from the orange into a blender, adding the pulp from the citrus squeezer, together with the ice cubes. Halve the papaya, discard the seeds, and scoop the flesh into the blender using a spoon. Blend until smooth, then stir in the seeds from the passion fruit. Mix briefly and serve in a glass.

strawberry shake

A filling smoothie to whip up for breakfast before you rush out the door and face the day.

3 ice cubes

¼ cup skim milk

¼ cup low-fat plain or strawberry yogurt

1¼ cups strawberries, hulled and chopped

½ banana, sliced

½ teaspoon pure vanilla extract

1 tablespoon honey

SERVES 1

Put all the ingredients in a blender and process until smooth. Pour into a glass and serve.

mango, raspberry, and orange smoothie

This is a great accompaniment to a couple of slices of whole-grain toast, a banana, or a bowl of cereal.

1 large orange

½ mango, peeled, pitted, and chopped

¾ cup fresh or frozen raspberries

3 ice cubes (if using fresh berries)

SERVES 1

Squeeze the juice from the orange and pour into a blender, adding the pulp from the citrus squeezer. Add the chopped mango, raspberries, and ice cubes, if using, and blend until smooth. Pour into a glass and serve.

pussyfoot

Pussyfoot is one of the best non-alcoholic drinks around, and greatly appreciated by designated drivers and pregnant women. It is very refreshing, thanks to the mellowing effect of the grenadine (sweet pomegranate syrup). Make sure the juices are freshly squeezed—carton juice will not do. Leave out the egg yolk if there's any risk involved—it won't matter greatly, you can always add a tablespoon of cream.

¼ **cup freshly squeezed orange juice**

2 tablespoons freshly squeezed lemon juice

2 tablespoons freshly squeezed lime juice

1–2 tablespoons grenadine

1 free-range egg yolk (optional)

ice cubes

SERVES 1

Pour the orange, lemon and lime juices, grenadine, and optional egg yolk into a cocktail shaker half-filled with ice cubes. Shake well and strain into a glass filled with more ice cubes.

Variation Add a dash of sparkling water or lemonade for bit of festive fizz.

homemade fresh lemonade

Fresh lemonade is simple to make, and if you keep the lemony syrup in the fridge, you have an almost instant drink to dilute with either chilled sparkling mineral water or soda water on a sweltering day.

finely grated peel and freshly squeezed juice of 6 large, juicy, unwaxed lemons

1 cup sugar

sparkling mineral water or soda water, chilled, to dilute

TO SERVE

ice cubes

fresh lemon slices

fresh mint sprigs

SERVES 6–8

Put the lemon peel, sugar, and 2½ cups water in a nonaluminum saucepan and bring slowly to a simmer, stirring to dissolve the sugar. As soon as the sugar has dissolved and the syrup begins to bubble, take it off the heat. Half cover and leave until cold.

Squeeze the lemons and add the juice to the cold syrup. Strain into a bowl, cover, and chill.

Serve in a glass pitcher with ice cubes, fresh lemon slices, and sprigs of mint, diluted with chilled sparkling mineral water or soda water on a ratio of about 1 part syrup to 1 part water.

Variation Add a small pinch of saffron threads to the warm syrup when you take it off the heat.

pear and ginger juice

12 oz. ripe pears, peeled, cored, and chopped

1 large orange, peeled and separated into segments

1 inch fresh ginger, chopped

2 tablespoons crushed ice, to serve (optional)

SERVES 2

Pear is very gentle on the digestive system and ginger is an effective remedy against nausea and travel sickness, so this is a great drink to take on journeys or to give to your child after a stomach upset.

Push the pears, orange, and ginger through a juicer. Put 1 tablespoon crushed ice, if using, in each of 2 tall glasses, pour the juice over the top, and serve.

apple and carrot juice

3 medium carrots, chopped

2 apples, peeled, cored, and chopped

2 tablespoons crushed ice, to serve (optional)

SERVES 2

This is high in soluble fiber, which is necessary for a healthy digestive system, and full of immune-boosting antioxidants.

Push the carrot and apple pieces through a juicer. Put 1 tablespoon crushed ice, if using, in each of 2 tall glasses, pour the juice over the top, and serve.

iced ginger tea

2 inches fresh ginger, peeled and finely sliced

4 tea bags (preferably Indian tea)

2 limes, sliced

ice cubes, to serve

lemonade, to serve

SERVES 6

When making iced tea, it's best to add the tea bags to cold water rather than boiling water in order to avoid the unpleasant scum that can appear on the surface. So boil the water, then let it cool before adding the tea.

Put the sliced ginger into a large pitcher, pour over 1 quart boiling water, and leave until cold. Add the tea bags and chill for 1 hour.

Strain the tea into a clean pitcher, add the slices of lime and ice cubes, then top up with lemonade.

iced lemon coffee

2 cups freshly brewed espresso coffee

sugar, to taste

ice cubes, to serve

1 tablespoon freshly squeezed lemon juice

6 twists of lemon peel, to serve

SERVES 6

Iced lemon coffee can be just as refreshing as iced lemon tea on a hot day. It may sound a little strange, but it's very thirst-quenching.

Pour the coffee into a large pitcher, add sugar to taste, and stir until dissolved. Let cool, then chill until very cold.

Half-fill 6 glasses with ice cubes. Add the lemon juice to the coffee, then pour into the glasses and serve with a twist of lemon peel.

moroccan mint tea

1½ heaping tablespoons green
tea leaves

a handful of fresh mint leaves
(not spearmint)

about ¾ cup sugar, or to taste

SERVES 6

Mint tea is very soothing after a spicy meal. Don't use spearmint—it will taste like mouthwash.

Heat a teapot with just-boiled water. Tip out the water, add the tea leaves, and pour a little boiling water over them just to moisten. Swirl around, then quickly pour the water out again, taking care not to lose any leaves. Add a good handful of fresh mint (the sugar is traditionally added at this stage, but leave it out or serve it later). Pour about 1 quart boiling water over the mint and moistened tea leaves. Put on the lid and let infuse for 5–8 minutes. Pour into warmed glasses and top with a few extra mint leaves. Hand the sugar around separately.

real hot chocolate

1½ oz. bittersweet chocolate,
finely chopped

1 teaspoon sugar

⅔ cup milk

TO SERVE (OPTIONAL)

whipped cream
mini-marshmallows

SERVES 1

Not a packet mix but the real thing—chocolate, milk, and a dash of sugar, plus whipped cream and mini-marshmallows if you really want to have fun.

Put the chocolate, sugar, and milk in a small saucepan. Heat up the milk until it is almost boiling. Stir occasionally with a wooden spoon to help the chocolate melt.

Remove the saucepan from the heat and put onto a heatproof surface. Using a rotary whisk, beat the milk until it is very smooth and foaming. Carefully pour the hot chocolate into a mug. Top with a swirl of cream (from a can, or whip some cream in a bowl with the rotary whisk) and sprinkle with a few mini-marshmallows, if using.

index

conversion charts

Weights and measures have been rounded up or down
slightly to make measuring easier.

A US stick of butter weighs 4 oz. which is approximately 115 g or
8 tablespoons.

Volume equivalents

American	Metric	Imperial
1 teaspoon	5 ml	
1 tablespoon	15 ml	
1/4 cup	60 ml	2 fl.oz.
1/3 cup	75 ml	2 1/2 fl.oz.
1/2 cup	125 ml	4 fl.oz.
2/3 cup	150 ml	5 fl.oz. (1/4 pint)
3/4 cup	175 ml	6 fl.oz.
1 cup	250 ml	8 fl.oz.

Weight equivalents

Imperial	Metric
1 oz.	25 g
2 oz.	50 g
3 oz.	75 g
4 oz.	125 g
5 oz.	150 g
6 oz.	175 g
7 oz.	200 g
8 oz. (1/2 lb.)	250 g
9 oz.	275 g
10 oz.	300 g
11 oz.	325 g
12 oz.	375 g
13 oz.	400 g
14 oz.	425 g
15 oz.	475 g
16 oz. (1 lb.)	500 g
2 1b.	1 kg

Measurements

Inches	cm
1/4 inch	5 mm
1/2 inch	1 cm
3/4 inch	1.5 cm
1 inch	2.5 cm
2 inches	5 cm
3 inches	7 cm
4 inches	10 cm
5 inches	12 cm
6 inches	15 cm
7 inches	18 cm
8 inches	20 cm
9 inches	23 cm
10 inches	25 cm
11 inches	28 cm
12 inches	30 cm

Oven temperatures

250°F	120°C	Gas 1/2
275°F	140°C	Gas 1
300°F	150°C	Gas 2
325°F	160°C	Gas 3
350°F	180°C	Gas 4
375°F	190°C	Gas 5
400°F	200°C	Gas 6
425°F	220°C	Gas 7
450°F	230°C	Gas 8
475°F	240°C	Gas 9

credits